OF EDUCATION, FISHBOWLS, AND
RABBIT HOLES

OF EDUCATION, FISHBOWLS, AND RABBIT HOLES

Rethinking Teaching and Liberal Education
for an Interconnected World

Jane Fried

with Peter Troiano

Foreword by
Dawn R. Person

1996–2016 20ᵀᴴ ANNIVERSARY

Stylus
PUBLISHING, LLC.

STERLING, VIRGINIA

Published by Stylus Publishing, LLC.
22883 Quicksilver Drive
Sterling, Virginia 20166-2102

Library of Congress Cataloging-in-Publication Data
Names: Fried, Jane, author.
Title: Of education, fishbowls, and rabbit holes : rethinking
teaching and liberal education for an interconnected world /
Jane Fried.
Description: First edition. | Sterling, Virginia : Stylus Publishing, LLC,
2016. | Includes bibliographical references and index.
Identifiers: LCCN 2015026438|
    ISBN 9781620364192 (cloth : alk. paper) |
    ISBN 9781620364208 (pbk. : alk. paper) |
    ISBN 9781620364215 (library networkable e-edition) |
    ISBN 9781620364222 (consumer e-edition)
Subjects: LCSH: Education, Higher--Philosophy. |
Education, Higher--Aims and objectives. | Education, Humanistic. |
Education and globalization.
Classification: LCC LB2322.2 .F74 2016 | DDC 370.11/2--dc23
LC record available at http://lccn.loc.gov/2015026438

13-digit ISBN: 978-1-62036-419-2 (cloth)
13-digit ISBN: 978-1-62036-420-8 (paperback)
13-digit ISBN: 978-1-62036-421-5 (library networkable e-edition)
13-digit ISBN: 978-1-62036-422-2 (consumer e-edition)

Printed in the United States of America

All first editions printed on acid-free paper
that meets the American National Standards Institute
Z39-48 Standard.

Bulk Purchases

Quantity discounts are available for use in workshops and for
staff development.
Call 1-800-232-0223

First Edition, 2016

10   9   8   7   6   5   4   3   2

This book is dedicated to Donna Fairfield, who taught me how to teach; to all my students, who told me when my teaching either was or was not very effective; to Burns B. Crookston, who knew about teaching, learning, and student development before anybody ever looked at a brain scan; and, finally, to the people who introduced me to Winnie the Pooh at an Early Age and allowed me to understand how Eeyore and Pooh could exist in the same Forest and be Friends despite their Differences in Perspective.

CONTENTS

Contents

D r. Jane Fried is a reflective scholar and educator who has taught and served as a student affairs administrator in higher education for over 40 years. She has experienced the massive infusion of technology, globalization, and internationalization of U.S. higher education as well as the disruptions that these developments have provoked. At the same time, our institutions have welcomed exceedingly diverse populations of new students who diverge by age, race, gender, geography, nationality, sexual orientation, learning style, and economic and personal challenges from previous generations of scholars. External and internal disruptions of the status quo led Fried to observe that, although our curricula have changed during this period, our pedagogical methods have become stagnant and increasingly ineffective over the past millennium.

Fried graduated from a liberal arts college in 1966. Her education profoundly shaped her view of the purposes of higher education as well as her view of the world. A child of the 1960s and a person whose earliest friends were African Americans and children of refugees from Europe, Fried is anchored in multiple realities as a woman. These multiple lenses give her access to many perspectives about the ways the world works. She believes that a major purpose of college attendance is to educate students to become functioning members of our democracy by learning to dialogue across perspectives and participate in addressing civic problems.

The first major theme of this book is that higher education in the United States is firmly anchored in a Eurocentric worldview. Most college faculty and staff see the world through this perspective and are not aware of the ways in which it shapes their interpretation of teaching and learning. Fried calls this perspective the "fishbowl," and asks us to look at (or deconstruct) our fishbowl, rather than simply looking through it and seeing what we assume to be singular truth. She uses the fishbowl metaphor to suggest that a limited lens such as the fish in the fishbowl is a destructive stance for higher education and learning, and that it will lead to a narrowing of perspectives and possibilities. Instead, Fried challenges us to remember the practices offered by adult educators such as Jack Mezirow and Paulo Freire who encouraged engagement in learning where the teacher is facilitator and student and teacher construct learning together. The learner brings much to the process of teaching and the teacher brings much to the process of learning.

The Eurocentric fishbowl incorporates the mind/body split. This separation of thinking from feeling has great utility in many areas of study but it often does not work in a classroom of diverse students who come from more integrated cultures. Fried struggled with her efforts to fuse thinking and feeling in classroom conversations so that students from all cultural backgrounds could become involved in meaningful learning. This struggle led to her realization that the mind/body split was a useful construct in research but does not accurately reflect the ways in which humans learn.

The second major theme is the need to incorporate what has been learned about learning, through cognition and neuroscience, into the ways that we teach in higher education. This theme pulls us "down the rabbit hole." The metaphor of a rabbit hole suggests that the changes in perspective lead to disorientation and confusion as we move past the Cartesian split toward an integrated understanding of self-authorship and learning. The idea of self-authorship and an increasing emphasis on general education are fundamental to her recommendations for change. The final measure of success lies in integrated assessment and evaluation, which reflects both accurate understanding of information and an ability to describe the value of the information in our complex world. The ways we organize knowledge for research and teaching purposes is not appropriate for helping students understand what they need to know in most disciplines. Neuroscience has reshaped our understanding of brain–based learning processes, and constructivism has begun to complement positivism in pedagogical philosophy and process. This idea is quite disorienting to those of us who have made careers of being experts. Very few of us remain expert in teaching because new understandings of learning are forcing us to question our fundamental teaching methods. Fried integrated all that she had come to know from her cognitive understanding of human development and the teaching and learning process with her observations of student learning and ability to use what they knew to improve her educational process with students.

When Fried began to create *Shifting Paradigms in Student Affairs* (Fried, 1995), she invited authors to write applied pieces that reflected the reality of daily practice and life of scholars from marginalized groups. She sought out contributors who were able to write about border crossings because they were living the experience in their professional and personal lives. Fried did not like or appreciate my contribution, which was my first piece of solo writing. She told me to write from my heart, not in the traditional academic impersonal voice, and to tell my story as only I could. She helped me find my voice as a scholar and writer. That is what this book is about. Fried is calling on each of us to find our own voice in the classroom and to listen and incorporate our students so that we become learners with them in the process of higher education. We need to help our students find their voices in this same process.

Fried suggests that the university is a central space for creating mental maps of our material and spiritual worlds, conceptual and emotional ways of knowing and theoretical and applied understanding. Students come to higher education to make sense of their lives in all these domains and are often frustrated with the purely impersonal and intellectual approaches used in many classrooms. To improve learning, teaching must become more holistic and encompass more the than traditional Western perspective. Using the fishbowl metaphor, she encourages storytelling in college that goes beyond the Grand Narrative and seeks the nonobjective realities reflective of insights that all students bring to the classroom. The values reflected in our teaching narratives need to be examined in relationship to the narratives of those we are teaching. Fried suggests that we need to be conscious of the manner in which we disseminate information, and we should be aware of the perspectives lost when we teach only what we can see or know. We overcome this limitation by inviting students to bring what they know into the classroom and by valuing their contributions as much as we value our own.

Fried asked the fundamental questions, which must be posed periodically to keep U.S. higher education in check: What is the purpose of higher education? Is it simply to perpetuate the status quo? Is it to transmit culture? Or, is it to train and prepare the masses for the world of work? Fried encourages us to think about what this means for us as a society and what the meaning and role of education is in an advanced technological world.

We cannot continue to do business as usual in higher education. Each time we lose a student from the educational process, we lose potential and capability to move us forward as a nation, community, and family. For example, the Census Bureau has reported that fewer than 10 of every 100 Latinos, one of the fastest growing populations in the United States, graduate from college with a four-year degree. We are failing many of our learners. We are at a point where academic learning needs to be integrated with social and emotional learning in order to support equity for all students.

This book adds perspective and opportunity for reflection for any teacher to consider. It speaks to the need for transformative curriculum leadership and the need to reconceptualize the curriculum. Henderson and Gornik (2006) wrote about the transformative curriculum emphasizing subject matter and the development of a democratic self for the learner and for social understanding. Much of what Fried advocates is also supported by transformative curriculum theory. *Curriculum theory* is defined as the interdisciplinary study of educational experiences in order to support the development of self-realization and moral responsibility to facilitate students' journeys of understanding. All of this supports the connection of the heart and soul with the mind for holistic learning and development. I cannot imagine a finer higher learning experience than one that encourages prisms rather than fishbowls.

Dawn R. Person
Professor, Department of Educational Leadership
Coordinator, Higher Education Graduate Programs
Director, Center for Research on Educational Access and Leadership
California State University, Fullerton

"If somebody teaches but nobody learns, what do you call that?" The inquisitive student who asked that question also answered it: "A lot of hot air." Although that question was posed and answered in my classroom by a student a long time ago, I have never forgotten it. The question seems absolutely fundamental to the higher education enterprise. Faculty members do a lot of teaching. What is teaching? Talking? Showing? Asking? Setting up electronic bulletin boards? Creating and evaluating problem sets, as they do at MIT (Carey, 2015)? What is the connection between teaching and learning? If students learn (assessed by whatever metric you choose), can we assume that teaching has occurred? No, I don't believe that we can. People learn all kinds of things without teaching, like walking, speaking, comparing, playing *ad infinitum.*

In the past several years faculty members have begun to ask ourselves, Why should students attend college, and what can we reasonably expect them to learn? The *evidence of learning,* defined as retention of information and the development of critical thinking over the long term, is spotty. Arum and Roksa (2011) have recently documented the failure of a significant percentage of college students to learn, let alone retain, the vast amounts of information to which they are exposed or to demonstrate the critical thinking abilities that are necessary to make sound judgments based on this information.

Students typically tell us that they attend college "to get a better job" or "to have a better life." If students aren't learning what we expect them to learn and the methods we are using to teach them are often ineffective, how do we justify the massive amount of human and material resources that the United States puts into the enterprise of higher education every semester?

I have been pondering this question for quite some time. Actually I have been going around in circles trying to come up with some reasonable understanding of this phenomenon since I began teaching more than 40 years ago. My circular thinking ended up taking me back to one of the first things I ever learned in my liberal arts education: To achieve a sense of mutual understanding in any conversation, it is critical to define the terms and examine the premises. Plato's myth of the cave kept coming to mind. Almost all of our educational reforms involve increased use of technology; more entertaining presentation of information; and skill development devoted to helping students take notes, increase time on task, and formulate good questions. We have been trying to improve our teaching methods without asking ourselves how people learn. The lightbulb came on in my mind. In Plato's myth, prisoners in a darkened cave are looking at shadows on the cave wall (illusions) and not looking directly at the phenomenal world in daylight. In focusing on techniques and technology, I believe we are doing the same thing. We are increasing the size of the shadows, building up the fire that throws the shadows, but we are not looking at the most important, real-world element of good teaching: understanding how human beings learn.

There has been a great deal of research on the brain and learning processes in the past 25 years. Almost none of this new information has been connected with techniques that can be used to improve teaching. In my circumambulations regarding this problem, I have concluded that because very little of the recently developed information about learning and brain function has been applied directly to the improvement of what we call teaching, some common definitions of those terms are crucial to progress in this conversation. We need to know what individuals mean when they use the terms *teach* and *learn* and if people who are using those terms in a conversation all mean the same thing. We need to realize that learning can occur without teaching, but when teaching happens and nobody learns, we are faced with a phenomenon that we can't explain except by blaming it on students. That student of long ago whom I quoted had a very good question. In this book I address that question in a broad historical and cultural context. I focus on teaching, learning, and the role of self in shaping knowledge and understanding. Including self in this discussion is a radical departure from the epistemology most of us learned in graduate school. What is contained in this text is rather disorienting for any traditionally trained academic in the Western world.

This book addresses several issues that I believe are significant in the redesign and restructure of the new American university (Crow & Dabars, 2015). To teach undergraduates effectively, we must do the following:

- Reexamine the purpose of education in the liberal arts and reframe it for the twenty-first century.
- Incorporate the new knowledge about learning that has been developed in cognitive science and neuroscience into our pedagogy.
- Move beyond the positivist paradigm of teaching and learning inherited from the German research universities and incorporate both constructivism and the role of emotions in learning into our pedagogy as indicated by the learning research.
- Construct a pedagogical approach that integrates cognition, affect, behavior, and reflection into standard methodology (Zull, 2002).
- Learn about the notion of *self-authorship* (Baxter-Magolda, 1999), and place it at the core of our work with students.
- Participate in professional development activities so that we can become skilled and competent in the use of these new ideas and methods.

I am assuming that any educator who understands how people learn can become highly skilled as a teacher in a discipline or as a trainer in any applied field. I have incorporated metaphors from *Alice's Adventures in Wonderland* and *Winnie the Pooh* in this book because I think any discussion that is disorienting or disconcerting should be entertaining as well. I invite you to follow me down the rabbit hole to a place where people learn what they care about, where emotions elucidate and anchor learning, and where people remember what they have learned because they know why it matters to them.

Conceptual Map

If you don't know where you're going, any road will take you there.

(Attributed to Lewis Carroll)

"He's out," said Pooh sadly. "That's what it is. He's not in.
I shall have to go a fast Thinking Walk by myself."

(Milne/Shepard, 1986, p. 32)

Terrain

The terrain of this book is broad and the journey is circular. In keeping with my references to children's stories such as *Alice's Adventures in Wonderland* and *Winnie the Pooh,* I explore the ways in which cultures use stories to help members of their group make sense of the world, learn the history of their people, and understand the various roles that members of this group are expected to play in the collective life of the group. The notion of storytelling is also called the Grand Narrative, the story that Western culture tells its members about how the world works. I also examine the story that seems to shape higher education in the West and look at some of the historical elements that have contributed to this story. These narratives are discovered to be accurate in some cases, inaccurate in others, and wildly misleading under certain circumstances. A closer examination of the elements of the narrative that pertain to teaching and learning ensues. After reviewing the story, I then explore the various teaching methods that faculty members in Western universities have used as well as cultural beliefs about valid teaching and learning or pedagogy and epistemology.

Guideposts

As a reader you will frequently be asked to take a look at your personal frame of reference within the Grand Narrative, the narrative of your career, and the narrative of your campus. The generic frame of reference is called the *fishbowl,* a phenomenon that shapes how we see the world even when we are not aware of the shaping process. To understand your frame of reference or perspective, you will need to stop reading, do some exercises and reflections, and critique your unexamined assumptions from new angles. The boxed exercises throughout this text are guide-posts to support the process. Be prepared for a bit of discomfort and disorientation.

Roadblocks

- *Preconceived Ideas About What Constitutes Legitimate Pedagogy and Academic Conversation in Colleges and Universities.* Ever since Descartes told us that thinking led to the most reliable form of knowing, we have been suspicious of including feelings or faith/intuition in academic conversations. We have a fairly narrow definition of *reliable knowledge* and a fairly narrow range of legitimate methods for discovering it. This belief is deeply embedded in us. Most of us have been trained to exclude knowledge that is influenced by feelings or faith from most academic discussions.
- *Talking About Feelings With Students.* Many of us (whoever you want to include in "us") believe that we shouldn't talk about feelings with students because we haven't been trained to do so. There is a widespread misconception that talking about feelings is the same thing as doing psychotherapy. Consider, however, that we often talk about feelings with people we care about. Educators who are uncomfortable having this kind of conversation with students need to understand the difference between an uncomfortable or emotionally upsetting conversation and a therapy session. Of course, if we work on campuses that have counseling centers, we need to know where they are and how to help students get that type of support when they need it.
- *Talking About Faith.* Separation of church and state means that no person or organization is permitted to impose a belief system on another. It does not mean that people cannot talk about faith. Faith in one form or another, not necessarily the religious form, is fundamental to human progress. Sarton (1973) implied in her *Journal of a Solitude* that faith is the fundamental force that motivates people to sustain hope, to achieve their dreams, and to persist through difficulty. "One must think like a hero to behave like a merely decent human being" (p. 101). In this era of first-generation students, there are increasing numbers of

people for whom faith is fundamental. Without it, they might not have enrolled in the first place. To get over this roadblock, listen carefully to students' expression of faith. It is not necessary to agree or disagree. The most important aspect of faith for students is in their own capabilities.

Destination

The destination for this journey is to Get Someplace Else. More specifically, it is to support educators in their journey toward understanding the connections among a person's sense of self (self-authorship), the ways the person learns, what the person wishes to learn, and how the person hopes to use what he or she learns to shape his or her own life. This is a difficult intellectual journal for any educator who has been trained in the Western Grand Narrative of objectivity and autonomy, or separation of self and feelings from knowing and thinking. This book includes a lengthy discussion about balancing transmission and evaluation of information with acknowledging variations on interpretive perspective and the feelings that result from different interpretations. The two appendices provide techniques for managing the fact/perspective/feeling/meaning vortex in conversations with students. How will you know if you've arrived, or even if you've made Progress? You will be more comfortable in your classes or encounters with students. You will remember why you decided to become an academic, the excitement when you first realized what you wanted to study and teach. Your teaching will become more creative and more interesting to you and your students. You will begin to care as much about the learning process as the content. You will be surprised.

About This Book

Chapter 1, "Teaching, Learning, and Storytelling," examines the stories that we tell ourselves about the purposes of college, why people attend, and what happens in these institutions. The chapter also covers subjectivity, objectivity, the mind/body split, and personal perspectives and narratives.

The Grand Narrative is the story a culture tells itself about how the world works. Chapter 2, "Life Beyond the Fishbowl: The Grand

Narrative, Academic Disciplines, and Deep Learning," examines the way the Grand Narrative of Western cultures shapes the ways we think about learning and teaching in theoretical and applied disciplines.

Learning is a constant process for all of us. Chapter 3, "Everybody Learns, Some Teach," delves into the questions, "How do we learn?" Is a teacher required? Do we teach the way people learn?

Is teaching something we do to students, with students or is it an interactive process that should also involve learning? Chapter 4, "Entr'acte: Is 'Teach' a Transitive Verb?," looks at the role of language in shaping commonly accepted ideas about teaching.

Chapter 5, "Self-Authorship: A New Narrative of Learning," discusses the importance of including the role of self in learning. The historical narrative of higher education has been that subject and object are separate and self is not a variable to be considered in learning. However, recent research indicates that the validity of this perspective is quite limited. Teaching as if the student's sense of self were irrelevant almost guarantees boredom and loss of information retention as soon as the test is over or the paper is written.

Chapter 6, "Professional Boundaries and Skills: Searching for Meaning Is Not Counseling," is an exploration of the differences between conversations that involve either emotional content or helping students struggle to make meaning of their experiences and counseling. They are not the same kinds of conversations, but the differences are typically not clear to laypeople. Most professors are advisers, not counselors in any professional sense. When students are struggling to understand why they should learn information in any discipline and how that knowledge might help them understand the broader context of their lives, they need advice from an experienced scholar and the opportunity to engage in a thoughtful conversation.

Why do so many students consider general education requirements obstacles to be overcome on the road to professional education? If we were to consider the role of self-understanding in the broader context of any aspect of general education, students would become more engaged with the subject matter and understand more of the value of the discipline. Chapter 7, "Curriculum, General Education, and the Grand Narrative," explores several alternative methods of organizing general education requirements that place the student in the larger cultural context of community, culture, and environment.

Assessment has often been considered a confusing and time-consuming process. Nevertheless, it has now become fundamental to every aspect of higher education. When you hear the term *metrics*, it means somebody wants an assessment of something as one factor in resource allocation. In chapter 8, "Assessment: Documenting Learning From Alternate Perspectives," Peter Troiano provides an introduction to the assessment process as well as references to additional resources.

I have also provided two appendices. "Appendix A: Working in Groups and Facilitating Discussions," introduces methods for using group process in an academic discussion. Resources for additional skills and techniques are also included. "Appendix B: Contemplative Practices for Classroom Use," provides contemplative methods for use in the classroom as well as in out-of-class activities. Additional resources from the Association for Contemplative Mind in Higher Education are also included.

ACKNOWLEDGMENTS

I would like to thank my dear friends and colleagues Alicia Fedelina Chávez and Susan Longerbeam for their extensive descriptions of the relationships among teaching, learning, and culture. In reading their recent book, *Teaching Across Cultural Strengths*, I have realized that this book is written in a "New York City, in-your-face" mode. I never knew it was a mode—I just thought it was my personality. I now realize in a much more powerful way how self shapes learning and teaching and how culture shapes self. For those readers whose cultures are grounded in non–New York City environments, I ask your forgiveness and understanding. I hope you find any offenses entertaining. I would also like to thank Laura DeVeau, Alicia Fedelina Chávez, and Jerry Sazama for their careful reading of the manuscript, which helped me move this document into the world of consensual reality and out of my own fishbowl.

INTRODUCTION

*O*f *Education, Fishbowls, and Rabbit Holes* is a book I have wanted to write for a very long time. The impetus for this book is the hybrid and frequently frustrating and confusing nature of my 45-year career in higher education. I graduated from a liberal arts college in the 1960s. I was an English major. It just doesn't get more "gen ed" or well rounded than that. At that time, career training as a focus of college was a lot less important than it is in this era. Making money was a far less pressing issue. Thanks to Nelson Rockefeller, then governor of New York, my tuition was $50 per semester. My classes were small. My professors were erudite. I went to a mediocre high school in a poor city. College was a dream come true. I finally had a chance to Think About Things and talk to Smart People (the practice of bizarre capitalizations comes from *Winnie the Pooh*, discussed under "Rabbits and Rabbit Holes"). I realized that I wasn't as smart as others thought I was, but that being around Smart People was a lot of fun. I was desperate to understand a world that seemed to be coming apart. My friends were getting drafted. My friends were getting stoned. As a female member of the residence hall staff, I didn't have the opportunity to get either drafted or stoned, but I lived in that atmosphere, which was tense, ecstatic, frightening. Abortions were illegal. Sex was available. One universal motto was, "If it feels good, do it." I did some of it; others did much more. Some went on acid trips and didn't come back the same way they left. I was in the honors program and it was as boring as high school. That made no sense to me. So finally I dropped out of honors so I could write more interesting and less traditional papers.

My senior thesis was titled *De Rerum Naturae:* On the Nature of Things (Fried, 1966). This was a standard title for many medieval writings, and it was the most comprehensive and arrogant title

I could think of. The subject was solar and lunar imagery in the poetry of Wallace Stevens. Solar imagery is a metaphor for reason and logic. Lunar imagery is a metaphor for imagination and emotion. One of the poems I discussed was "How to Live. What to Do" (Stevens, 1964). I thought that pretty much covered the subject of the meaning of life, which is what I was trying to understand. I was searching for a balance between reason and emotion. I still am. Creating that balance was what I couldn't do in the honors program. I had to write analyses of poetry in the traditional/impersonal manner of outstanding scholars on their way to doctoral programs.

So, because I didn't want to or couldn't become excellent at impersonal analysis of poetry, I concluded that I wasn't as smart as I needed to be if I wanted to become a professor. But I loved being in college. It was the most fun I'd ever had in school. I was a newspaper editor, a judicial board member, a writer, and an overall student leader. But, if I wasn't smart enough to be a professor, what should I do to stay in college? That question is one that many of my colleagues have faced. We chose the emerging profession of student affairs because it allowed us to stay on campus and continue to do the work we loved, and it kept us out of the classroom, with its demands for endless writing on impersonal subjects.

I became a trainer. I taught resident assistants (RAs) how to become peer counselors. In this context there was no academic credit and my students had little intrinsic motivation to excel in the "RA course"; it was a job requirement for them. I had to develop a teaching style that combined experiential learning, trust building, stand-up comedy, and the ability to connect counseling and developmental theory for the purposes of helping college students succeed in school and make good choices in their lives. The problem has always been that training is not considered equivalent to teaching in higher education. Although teaching counseling skills to RAs did not involve academic credit, I realized that what these students learned in terms of listening, decision making, and relationship building would stand them in good stead for the rest of their lives. Even if what I did wasn't called teaching, nobody could deny that the students learned very important life skills.

And that brings us to the Rabbit Hole. In the ensuing 45 years a great deal of research on learning has been conducted. It turns out that people learn only what they care about, subjects that have personal meaning for them and are in some way related to their own lives beyond the classroom. Unfortunately, a great deal of higher learning, particularly the liberal arts, is based on the notion that emotions interfere with learning, and in many cases, connecting personal meaning and factual information simply confuses things. Barry Goldwater ran for president while I was in college. One of his mottos was, "In your heart you know he's right." One of my friends used to counter, "But in your head you know he's wrong." The problem is that you can't know only with your head or with your heart. These two organs, physically and metaphorically, have to speak with each other if you really want to "know" something. This is now scientific fact as well as instinctive understanding. You can feel it in your heart. You can express it in metaphors. You can also see it on a functional magnetic resonance imaging (fMRI) scan.

Descartes articulated his famous statement "I think, therefore I am" in 1637. This aphorism generally conveys the notion that the only trustworthy knowledge is cognitive knowledge. The phrase and its implied epistemology has provided the foundation for Western science, leading researchers to the scientific method in which empiricism, thinking about objective reality, is the only form of knowing that is considered valid and reliable in many of the academic disciplines. Descartes, like Newton, was correct, but not comprehensive. His approach supported sound rational thinking as the West emerged from Church-based descriptions of reality to empirical descriptions. Einstein pushed us past Newton, and the current group of neuroscientists who study learning have pushed us beyond Descartes. Realizing that people learn most effectively and profoundly when thinking, feeling, acting, and constructing personal meaning are all integrated is profoundly disorienting for many academics. Most professors are used to teaching about the world in an empirical, objective manner and not used to discussing feelings or personal meaning. In fact, bringing these perspectives into the classroom is often considered inappropriate and irrelevant.

Finally, as I reach the end of my academic career, I understand why I thought I wasn't too bright and why my professors didn't know what to do with my insistence that meaning and feeling had to be included in the conversation. I just couldn't split up thinking, feeling, and the implications of the reflection and analysis on my own anticipated future and current behavior. Without the whole picture of knowing, as I then intuited it, learning was as boring as dirt. This attitude didn't bode well for an academic future.

Themes, Terminology, and Reader Engagement

This book was written almost in stream of consciousness style. Thanks to several very good friends and colleagues, we did manage to pull out many of the kinks so that the text flows more smoothly. The book is more like a workshop than a written document in that it is filled with stories, my reflections, and requests for the reader to reflect on his or her own personal history or current beliefs. All of these aspects are designed to contribute to a "whole learning" experience, engaging heart, mind, and meaning. There are several themes that run throughout the book. Within each theme are exercises designed to engage readers in personal explorations of some aspect of the theme. Following is a brief explanation of these themes.

The Grand Narrative of the West. The Grand Narrative is the broad story of the world and how it works as commonly understood by people who come from or whose ancestors came from Northern Europe, particularly the areas where the Enlightenment arose. The Grand Narrative as it is referenced in this book is generally derived from *The Cave and the Light* (Herman, 2013), *The Great Work* (Berry, 1999), and *The More Beautiful World Our Hearts Know Is Possible* (Eisenstein, 2013). References to the Grand Narrative appear frequently, and the major ideas included in the narrative are listed and discussed. This narrative is currently under pressure to change, but because it is so large and comprehensive, it changes slowly and almost imperceptibly. It is also referred to as the fishbowl.

Personal Narrative. The personal narrative is the story that each individual uses to make sense out of the world. Personal narratives are typically derived from families; from ethnic, racial, and faith groups; and from the ways that the individual has constructed meaning in his or her life. These narratives change more quickly. Changes in narrative are typically upsetting or confusing. One of the major narratives for Americans is the subject of race, its construction and its significance. Both the Grand and the personal elements of this narrative are changing and affecting each other at the current time. People from cultures outside the United States and people from nondominant cultures within often have different narratives or a mix of narratives depending on context.

Self-Authorship. Self-authorship is the notion that attitudes toward authority change as people mature. Young children naturally rely on authority figures to tell them what to do, who to be, what to value, how to treat others, how to make choices, and so on. As children grow older they learn to rely more and more on their own judgment. Ultimately, Kegan defines *self-authorship* as "internally coordinating one's beliefs, values and interpersonal loyalties rather than depending on external values, beliefs and interpersonal loyalties" (as cited in Baxter Magolda & King, 2004, p. 18). Baxter Magolda and King assert that self-authorship has "three core assumptions about learning: knowledge is complex and socially constructed, one's identity plays a central role in crafting knowledge claims, and knowledge is mutually constructed via the sharing of expertise and authority" (p. xix). Fundamentally, these authors believe that self-authorship promotes the core task of learning in college. I concur. Self-authorship combines learning about the external world, learning about self, and learning about the creation of authoritative systems of interpreting world events. The modification to the notion of self-authorship that I am suggesting is an expanded definition of *self* so that it includes individuals, as in Euro-American culture, and people who define *self* in the context of group; as in Native, Latino, Asian, and African cultures.

Rabbits and Rabbit Holes. There are two very different rabbits in this text: Rabbit from *Winnie the Pooh* (Milne, 1926/1954) and the White Rabbit from *Alice's Adventures in Wonderland* (Carroll, 1865/1993). Pooh's Rabbit is a Fluffy Sort of a Rabbit who is Easily Confused but Very Accommodating. The White Rabbit is a Very Important Rabbit who has responsibilities in a royal entourage, is always behind schedule, and lives in an Alternate Reality. Pooh's Rabbit is in this book for Comfort and Reassurance. The White Rabbit is the creature who entices Alice to go down the Rabbit Hole, where she discovers that nothing is as she had thought it was and where the rules change constantly. A significant group of creatures live down the Rabbit Hole, and Alice is expected to interact with them appropriately. However, she has a great deal of difficulty trying to understand their expectations about appropriateness. The White Rabbit is rude and imperious and generally does not require capitalized words. White Rabbits are everywhere in higher education. They create processes like Learning Outcomes, Rubrics, Assessments, Common Cores, and a range of practices referred to as metrics. They always have rules, but these rules are not always understandable or predictable or even Sensible.

Questions That Keep Coming Up. Reading this book is like watching a Polaroid photograph develop (for those of you who remember those self-developing pictures). Questions come up repeatedly but never seem to be fully answered. Nevertheless, every time a question comes up, more detail is added. I frequently remark that we are now coming back to the original question. I do this because we need to keep exploring a few of those questions. There are some questions that have definitive answers, but those are not the questions that this book raises. So we keep coming back. Remember, I began by searching for the meaning of life. I am now asking the question, "What do students need to know, why do they need to know it, and how can we help them learn it?" I keep circling around the question looking for Rabbit Holes, more depth, and some eternally hidden wisdom that I am convinced is there, wherever there is.

Reader Engagement. This text has two different types of text boxes. One type contains stories from students or my own experience as a faculty member. The other has sets of questions for the reader to consider. A basic premise of this book is that learning is personal and requires time for reflection. These boxes and activities are designed to encourage you to pause for reflection. There are no quizzes, although you may find yourself sorely tested from time to time.

There are also two appendices. One discusses the dynamics of classroom conversations and contains examples of conversations that demonstrate facilitation skills to be used by the instructor. The other is a description of approaches to conducting contemplative exercises with students as part of helping them learn to reflect, to imagine long-term consequences, and to access their own insights, which may have been suppressed in other kinds of learning experiences. Contemplative practices generally have the effect of increasing self-authorship because they give students time to consider their own opinions about the subjects they are studying.

I

TEACHING, LEARNING, AND STORYTELLING

Nothing is as it appears, but we think that we see what is. What's that about? (Jane Fried, 1995)

We must become the storytellers of a new world. We tell the story not only with words but also with actions that spring from that story.

(Eisenstein, 2013, p. 203)

Storytelling . . . an activity reserved for leisure time. Images come to mind like playing with children, sitting around a campfire, or entertaining ourselves on a long winter evening with friends or family. Storytelling involves fiction, events created as much to entertain and interest as to inform. Stories change as they are passed along among tellers and listeners and over time. Stories often have instructional intent, particularly morality tales, but the moral is always embedded in a convoluted sequence that pulls the listener in by appealing to the emotions.

In contrast, we generally don't think of colleges and universities as places where stories are told or where they are part of the curriculum, except in literature courses. The presumptive role of higher education is to transmit empirical knowledge—use it to solve problems, maintain distance between emotions and information, and train people in the various empirically based skills that will prepare them for the

1

workforce. The places for telling stories in college are at parties, in residence halls, and in other areas of student life where empirical accuracy may not be the focus and conviviality is a higher priority. Nevertheless, stories in college and about college abound and are often unrecognized. For example, these stories are supported by students:

- The main reason to go to college is to get a better job or make more money.
- The main reason go to a particular college is its sports teams, social life, or the fact that everybody in a family has attended that college.
- The main reason to go to a particular college is that there are more men than women there or vice versa or that the campus is supportive of gay, lesbian, bisexual, and transgender students.
- The main reason to go to a particular college is that the student wants to study something specific and will follow through with that interest and the institution has a particularly strong program in that area.

Stories generally supported by faculty members include the following:

- The purpose of college is to train students to become critical thinkers.
- The purpose of college is to train students for a career.
- Academic research should exclude researcher bias to the greatest degree possible.
- Truth (or empirical accuracy) can be discerned by using "gold standard" research methods that exclude researcher bias, which can also be described as researcher perspective.
- Valid research generates information that can be considered reliable regardless of time or context.
- The role of faculty members is to communicate reliable knowledge to students and to assess their ability to repeat and apply this knowledge in periodic assessments (tests, lab demonstrations, performances, etc.).
- Students aren't as good/motivated/honest as they were when the faculty member was in school.

Why call these beliefs *stories?* These narratives are creative ways in which members of different groups weave together empirical information and anecdotal impressions to create a more or less orderly understanding of the world in which they are functioning. Educational psychologist Charles Ogbu described *culture* as "an understanding that people have of their universe that guides their interpretation of events as well as their expectations and actions in that universe" (as cited in Fried, 2012, p. 63). Stories shape the ways that culture expresses itself and help to create the norms of behavior within the group that subscribes to each story. People tell each other stories as a means to enculturate new members of a group and reinforce existing norms and history of the group among long-standing members. For example, Do you remember when we climbed to the top of the water tower, got so drunk we didn't know how we got back to campus, had the president who went to every athletic event drunk? Do you remember when people got tenure for writing letters to the editor? What is it about alcohol and college mythology? Perhaps this is another story for another time, or perhaps it's part of our weave of stories.

Higher Education as Culture and Subcultures: Stories That Go On and On

> *I think. Therefore I am.*
> *(Descartes)*

Berry (1999) credits Descartes with "desouling" the Western world. More accurately, Descartes separated body from soul in his philosophical system and convinced people that the only elements of awareness that were reliable were those about which one could think. Descartes excluded knowledge gleaned from awareness of emotions or intuition as valid knowledge. Across the range of human belief systems, people may or may not be considered to have or be souls. In some systems souls include many people and people are considered to be expressions of a larger soul. Opinions about animal souls vary. In the Western system inanimate objects are generally considered not to have souls; they are objects. In Eastern and Indigenous belief systems everything that exists has some kind of spiritual essence (Berry, 2009). The most comprehensive belief about souls is that the universe is one being, the Gaia hypothesis (Lovelock, 2009), and soul shapes all phenomena and interactions among elements of the universal being.

The Aboriginal people of Australia believe that stories and songs of the soul bring the world into existence. People sing the stories of their lives from birth to death. People of European descent generally believe that things are as they are, available to perception, but not shaped by the perceiver. Higher education stories are embedded in the story of Western culture as it has been spun since Greco-Roman antiquity, Biblical times, the Renaissance, and more particularly since the industrial/scientific revolution.

The story goes something like this:

- Autonomy is one of the highest human values. People are separate from each other and have the right to determine their own stories and shape their own destinies.
- Subject and object are separate. People act on the world. This is more or less a unidirectional process. The structure of the English language reflects this approach: subject-verb-object. In English, another person can be an object. In Mandarin and Japanese, people shape context as part of an interactive process. (Language structure and its effects on this story are discussed in chapter 4.)
- The separation of subject and object is fundamental to the Western way of perceiving and living in the world. The world is "out there," and people cause things to happen in the world by engaging in actions that change the world. The Western worldview privileges exteriority over interiority although there are rich traditions of mysticism and interiority in Christianity and Judaism (Berry, 2009).
- Logic, reason, and/or critical thinking represent the highest, most comprehensive and accurate level of understanding the world, other people, and all the social, biological, economic, and physical systems in which we live. This kind of thinking presumes the subject/object split. People don't just think. They have to think about something, preferably something external. Thinking about yourself, your feelings, your worries and hopes is often considered selfish or narcissistic. In college, students presumably learn to think about problems and issues in the

external world. In most Eastern belief systems, such as Tao, Hinduism, and Buddhism, thinking about yourself and your mental states is a highly valued, systematic form of inquiry that leads to inner peace, self-regulation, and compassion.

- Material reality is the only reliable form of reality and generally the preferred reality. Things are the most important thing. If it can't be counted and touched, then it isn't considered real. This belief leads to the concepts of ownership, accumulation, and wealth as the preferred state of being, and the notion that using various "metrics" will give us the most complete picture of learning. The more things a person owns, the better for the person and the person's status in the culture.

Recognizing Cultural Beliefs: It All Seems So Normal . . .

> *The prologues are over. It is a question now*
> *Of final belief. So say that the final belief*
> *Must be in a fiction. It is time to choose. (Stevens, 1964, "Oboe," p. 250)*

What do all these belief systems have to do with the way we organize higher education and thinking about teaching and learning? The Grand Narrative of Western culture (which is much more extensive and complex than the short description I have provided) shapes higher education. The Grand Narrative gives us, as Western people, a sense of how the world works and what we need to know to function effectively in this world. Deciding how to organize our social, educational, and economic systems is derivative of this set of beliefs (Eisenstein, 2013).

The story we tell ourselves about teaching, learning, and higher education goes like this:

- Because subject and object are separate, objectivity is the preferred way to approach teaching and learning. Objectivity is not considered problematic so no one raises the question about the validity of this particular mode of inquiry in a specific situation. It is assumed that valid inquiry and the knowledge we acquire should not be connected to personal perspectives, context, values, or feelings. In fact, the more we get emotionally involved with learning, the more confused we get. This approach may or may not be effective depending on what a person is learning or teaching, so a more effective or accurate approach might be to ask: When is objectivity more valuable and when is it less valuable if a person is trying to understand some phenomenon or develop insight?

- Autonomy and independence are essential. Students should be able to think independently, make life choices without being reliant on the support of others (Chickering & Reisser, 1993), and act on their own beliefs and judgments. Good judgments should be made on the basis of facts and not swayed by feelings. Autonomy in this context presumes separation and individuation. Alan Watts (1969) referred to the Western sense of self as an ego encased in a bag of skin. He made the Western construction of self visible. We are now aware that selves of Western derivation are separate and those of other cultural derivations are more connected to other people and to their myths of the cosmic universe.

- Student development or maturation is generally unrelated to classroom learning. Learning is cognitive, more or less predictable, and can be documented and assessed in uniform ways. Maturation is psychosocial, developmental, interpersonal, unpredictable, and often problematic. Learning in the classroom is orderly, and psychosocial learning is disorderly and far less predictable.

- Beliefs about soul, spirit, faith, and compassion are fundamentally outside the domain of higher education. These beliefs, whether they are embodied in formal religious practice or not, are private matters in a liberal democracy. People are free to believe whatever they wish in this domain, but these beliefs generally should not impinge on learning in public institutions.

Why Call This Belief System a Story? What Is Your Perspective on Perspectives?

Seeing is believing. (American adage)

Believing is seeing. (Fried, 2012, p. 19)

We are free to choose our perspective even when we are not free to challenge the consensual definition of the *facts*. One might ask this question: "Out of the infinite number of data bits and information available on a particular subject, how does one close borders between the pieces, separate them, and decide which ones are facts?"

Wallace Stevens (1964) wrote that the final belief "Must be in a fiction. It is time to choose" (p. 250). This does not mean that people need to create idiosyncratic explanations of the ways the world works, although sometimes that happens. It means that a basic element of human cognition is to create belief systems, hypotheses about cause and effect, and general meaning-making frameworks to explain sequences of events and purposes for action (Fried, 2012). "The purpose of organisms is to organize and what human beings organize is meaning. Meaning making is the activity of composing a sense of connections among things: a sense of pattern, order, form and significance" (Parks, 2000, p. 19).

What do you believe about beliefs and the ways they affect perception, interpretation, and action? The reason I have introduced here so many contrasting beliefs about the ways the world works is that I want to highlight the role of belief in shaping every element of human life. In the case of this book, our beliefs about teaching, learning, and organizing educational institutions shape everything we do with and for our students, our colleagues, and ourselves. Two obvious problems now come to mind: First, our entire system of teaching and learning was created when Newtonian physics framed our understanding of the world. The invention of "fuzzy logic," the Internet, and functional magnetic imagery has shown us a great deal about how the physical world and the brain work and how we learn. Newton's view was accurate but limited. Second, our belief system tells us that beliefs don't matter when it comes to learning and teaching. We believe that reality is out there, to be perceived. We don't pay any attention to the role of preconceived ideas or brain function in shaping what we think we know or perceive. What a conundrum.

Following are some of the beliefs that led to conclusions that were discovered to be misleading, inaccurate, or dangerous in recent history:

- A woman may become confused if her uterus gets loose from its attachments to her pelvis and starts migrating toward her brain. This was Freud's explanation for a variety of what he called hysterical disorders in women, including blindness and paralysis.

- The color of a person's skin and the configuration of the person's facial features affect intelligence. This is now known as racism.
- The ability to suppress emotions and make good judgments is a biologically determined characteristic typical of men. This is now described as sexism.
- Strength is shown by the ability to suppress emotions. This is now often considered high-stress behavior and can lead to high blood pressure, heart disease, and stroke.
- Women with blond hair are not typically as intelligent as people with darker hair.
- It is possible to infer many of a person's characteristics by the shape of and bumps in the person's skull. This was known as phrenology.
- Jews and Gypsies are inferior races and should be eliminated, the basis of Nazism and other forms of harassment and discrimination, still prevalent in some parts of Europe.
- People who are emotionally or physically attracted to members of the same sex are psychiatrically disturbed. This condition may be (a) a choice, (b) a sin, or (c) permanent.
- Corporations are people. This idea is currently in flux because of legal and logical concerns.

Becoming Aware of Beliefs and Wondering Where They Lead Us

So, if the final belief must be in a fiction, and if there are thousands of beliefs that individuals and cultures use to shape their ways of being and acting in the world, it is time to start asking ourselves: Are beliefs that shape our educational institutions taking us where we want to go and giving us the capacities that we need to function in our crisis-ridden world? The short answer is obviously no. An explanation of a longer inquiry and suggestions for some things you might want to do about it is the purpose of the rest of this book.

Pause for objections . . .

- Stop reading and make a list of everything you object to or disagree with about the previous set of assertions.
- Ask yourself: Where are the citations and why aren't there more of them?
- Tell yourself that some or little or none of this is true about the way you think or teach.
- Does doing this make you feel better? If so, you are looking at the world from the framework described.
- You might want to take a break right now.

2

LIFE BEYOND THE FISHBOWL

The Grand Narrative, Academic Disciplines, and Deep Learning

The Story of the World or the Story of the People is a matrix of narratives, agreements, symbolic systems that comprises the answers that our culture offers to life's most basic questions. . . . The narrative of the normal.
(Eisenstein, 2013, pp. 3–4)

The Grand Narrative goes by many names. The Grand Narrative of Western civilization is one way of describing the story we tell ourselves about how the world works and how we should expect our involvement in our world to evolve. The Grand Narrative shapes Western culture. It frames our ideas about how things work in the way a fishbowl shapes a fisheye view of the universe. We can see through the fishbowl, but we never exactly look at the bowl itself and ask ourselves if there is another way to perceive life beyond the bowl.

Sometimes we think the fishbowl view is the entire universe. Eisenstein (2013) calls this "the narrative of normal" (p. 3). The narrative of normal for those in higher education includes the following:

- The allegiance to "objectivity" as a way of knowing.
- The assumption that subject perceives, but generally does not interact with, object.
- The separation of people from each other through concepts of individuality and autonomy.

- The fundamentally material nature of the universe.
- The separation of spirituality and materialism.
- The inappropriateness of discussing spiritual issues in most academic disciplines.
- The assumption that human beings have rights but that these rights do not generally extend to other living things or to the planet itself.
- The assumption that a major, if not sole, purpose of attending college is for students to learn career-related skills that will allow them to earn a good living (materially) by working in fields that are based on most of the aforementioned assumptions.
- The assumption that a major role of faculty is to ensure that students learn and can use these skills in work settings.
- The assumption that students are generally between the ages of 18 and 24 with limited life experience. They often make decisions that harm themselves or others. It is generally not the role of faculty to get involved in this decision-making process or to help students examine the consequences of this behavior.
- The assumption that all things that students do outside the classroom are the responsibility of themselves or other adults employed in the university for purposes of helping students manage their lives (aka student affairs professionals).

From my 45 years of experience in higher education as both a student affairs professional and an academic faculty member, I believe that pretty much sums up the way we see things.

The Narrative of Your Current Experience

Put the book down. Close your eyes. Take yourself through an entire day of your life on your campus.

- Review your activities and the pleasures and pressures you feel.
- Ask yourself where elements of the Narrative of Higher Education shape what you do, what you value, and what you avoid.

- Are you focused on your own achievements and progress in your career (i.e., writing, acquiring grants, doing research, getting promoted)?
- Is there never enough time to get everything done because your environment is so fragmented?
- Are you more focused on knowing your students or knowing your discipline? Do you see these two elements of knowing as fundamentally different?
- Where does your family and personal life fit into your day/week?
- Do you ever share any elements of your personal life or concerns with your students?

How This Fishbowl Developed

Before the 1890s academic faculty taught, advised students, and managed institutions of higher education. In the European continental tradition, these were the only functions of faculty members, and students were responsible for managing the rest of their lives. In the English tradition, faculty members had the same responsibilities with an additional focus on faith and character development. This focus was grounded in the origins of these colleges as seminaries beginning with the founding of Oxford around 1100. Students at English schools were also considerably younger than their counterparts on the continent. Evidence of this English seminary tradition can still be seen in the requirement that students attend chapel in British public schools and many elite private schools in the United States. Higher education in the United States represents an awkward combination of these two traditions and varies drastically from institution to institution (Carey, 2015). The first dean of men, LeBaron Briggs, assumed his role at Harvard College in 1890. Alice Freeman Palmer became the first dean of women at the University of Chicago in 1892. The purpose of these offices was to handle the problems of student life, which were already getting beyond the interests and competencies of academic faculty. In the 1890s, the European research model for universities was encroaching on the earlier English model, demanding that faculty conduct research in the material sciences particularly and spend far less time concerning themselves with student life. Thus was a new field of activity developed, student affairs and services (Yoakum, 1919).

Why Do I Need to Know This?

The ways we teach, conduct research, and manage the lives of our institutions are a product of historical development and a fishbowl perspective. Readings (1996) described the university as the last institution in the modern world except for the church that bases its purpose and processes on unquestioned assumptions about singular, monotheistic Truth and Mission. As such, universities are not much inclined to look at their own fishbowl.[1] Many subcomponents of our institutions regularly examine their purposes, particularly in relation to what kinds of research to conduct and how to find funding for that research. However, the fundamental mission of most of our universities—the creation, transmission, and application of knowledge—has not changed in eons. This mission was set out in the Morrill Act of 1890, which provided funding to all states for the purpose of establishing universities to teach the mechanical, agricultural, and military sciences to a broad range of citizens to ensure wider opportunities for employment. Teaching the liberal or classical curriculum was an afterthought. Prior to the passage of the Morrill Act and the Industrial Revolution, less attention was paid to creation of knowledge and more to transmission of what was already known. Immanuel Kant (1798/1979) invented the one model of the modern university for Bismarck in a work called *Conflict of the Faculties*. The purpose of the modern, industrial, bureaucratic university was to produce bureaucrats for the emerging nation-states (i.e., managers of the modern corporation as well as governments) and to train people to "create knowledge for emerging industry that was based on the application of scientific information to industrial problems" (as cited in Fried, 2012, p. 4).

Let's take a look at our fishbowl. If we know the historical context in which our fishbowl was formed, we are in a better position to understand our lives as faculty, the ways our institutions function, and the values they seem to embody. Consider faculty salaries. The people in the applied areas of business and the professions are generally paid more than those in the liberal arts. Facilities in the former disciplines are more modern and sophisticated. But the liberal arts don't require a fancy room to sit around and talk. It doesn't even matter if the room is adequately heated or the ventilation is healthy. In some cases faculty and students in the liberal arts are treated less well than research animals and computer chips. Students generally do not understand what the purpose of studying the liberal arts subjects might be because there are no obvious practical implications and certainly no obvious employment possibilities. *Gen ed*, the term typically applied to liberal arts requirements, is usually considered a set of obstacles to be overcome in the journey toward the applied majors. Students often comment that they need to get their gen ed requirements out of the way. My favorite student comment of all time is, "What's a humanity and can I take it at 4 p.m.?" (personal communication, October, 2003). This student had a lot of responsibilities and no time for frills like poetry or art. The significant exception to this contra–gen ed mindset is psychology, because it has a very practical application for students who hope to understand themselves. It is clear from this method of creating academic requirements and allocating financial resources that the career-oriented fields are doing better than the fields in which the subject of character development and personal meaning-making might be discussed. The ways in which we organize our institutions, pay and reward our faculties, and allocate institutional resources all reflect our fishbowl perspective, which values practicality, applicability, materiality, and measurability and devalues philosophy, reflection, insight into personal issues, and the creation of adult value systems. This configuration of values and practices shapes our everyday lives, and we are often unaware of its influence.

Getting Out Of the Fishbowl

This fishbowl perspective is fundamentally monocultural and based on the perspectives described earlier. It is supported and shaped by two essential elements, monotheism and positivism; that is, One God and one accurate way to understand the physical world. Looking for the singular right answer is a characteristic of most elements of our educational systems and has been powerfully reinforced by the high-stakes testing movement that has been in vogue for the past decade. The God of this movement seems to appear in the form of the bubble sheet. Answers B and C on the bubble sheet may both have elements of accuracy, but one answer is preferred and is assumed to be correct.

There are at least three different perspectives from which to understand our fishbowl: (a) cognitive/developmental psychology (Kegan, 1994), (b) positivist/constructivist epistemology, and (c) a set of constructs around the ways that culture shapes our ideas about epistemology and pedagogy (Chávez & Longerbeam, 2016). From the perspective of cognitive/developmental psychology our early thinking divides the world into dichotomies, a philosophy broadly referred to as *dualism*. We see no gray areas. We believe that there are only two choices in any situation and that we should try to choose the right one. The other one is inevitably wrong (Perry, 1968). Our thinking typically becomes more complex as we mature. Perry documented the increasing development of complex thought among male college students as they progressed through their experiences at Harvard University in the 1950s. His students moved from *dualism* to *relativism,* in which they saw a range of interpretations of data but had little understanding about methods for deciding which data were more valid, to *commitment in relativism,* in which they realized that choices had to be made despite ambiguity, but that criteria could be developed on which to evaluate the choices. Belenky, Clinchy, Goldberger, and Tarule (1986) extended Perry's work through studying the same developmental processes with women. They found the same increasing complexity of thought, although their work with women also documented some differences in female ways of understanding and relying on their own perspective. These two theories are widely used by student affairs professionals to assess the developmental state of college students and create an advising perspective that both matches and challenges student points of view.

Using a philosophical lens, the ontological assumptions of both positivist and constructivist epistemologies provide insight. *Positivism* fundamentally asserts that valid information about the physical world can be apprehended through the senses and that credible perspectives will be consistent. Colloquially, "seeing is believing." When two people see the same event there is a presumption of universal and accurate perception. Both perspectives should see the same evidence. Our jury system is based on this assumption. Classical scientific research is also based on the same idea. *Constructivism* generally rejects the idea of truth without acknowledging the perspective from which the evidence to support truth is selected. Constructivism rejects the idea of a universal perspective and the discovery of facts in favor of the selection of facts from context with an acknowledgment of perspective (Code, 1993). For people who see through the fishbowl, perspective is not an issue. The fishbowl perspective is reality. For people to get beyond the fishbowl they have to know that it is shaping their vision and be able to imagine that there are other perspectives beyond the fishbowl that will yield different understandings of shared realities.

Finally, we should begin to think about the ways in which culture constructs our ideas and behavior as they are related to teaching, learning, and making sense of new information (Chávez & Longerbeam, 2016). Cultures can be described as falling along a continuum from individuated to integrated. *Individuated cultures,* such as those that have shaped approaches to teaching and learning in Europe and North America, expect members to believe that they are operating independently of each other, think in a linear fashion, and pay little attention to the context in which their behavior occurs. This cultural paradigm is valued and other perspectives are devalued. *Integrated cultures* expect members to believe that they are interdependent, that context should be constantly in their awareness, and that their thinking should shift focus between action and context in a cycle of reflection. Table 2.1 outlines the major elements of comparison between teaching and learning in individuated and integrated cultures.

It is typical on most campuses in the United States to have students from several of the cultures described in Table 2.1 sitting in the same classroom. A quick review of the typical teaching style for educators in almost any American college provides evidence that our "traditional" approach is governed by the culturally individuated approach and generally devalues the integrated approach. This unacknowledged fishbowl penalizes students from more integrated cultures who basically have to learn a new language of teaching and learning before they can begin to learn content. Students from integrated cultures tend to learn better with "hands-on" methods and appreciate having the opportunity to create or think about examples and being allowed or expected to discuss what they are learning with others who can provide different

Table 2.1 Differences between teaching and learning in individuated and integrative cultures.

Cultural Constructs in Teaching and Learning		
Individuated *In a culturally <u>individuated</u> framework, a private compartmentalized, linear, contextually independent conception of the world is common, assumed, and valued.*	⟷	**Integrated** *In a culturally <u>integrated</u> framework, an interconnected, mutual, reflective, cyclical, contextually dependent conception of the world is common, assumed, and valued.*
Knowledge, individual competence, to move forward toward goals and the betterment of humanity	**Purpose of Learning**	Wisdom, betterment of the lives of those with whom we are connected
Mind as primary, best, or only funnel of knowledge	**Ways of Taking in and Processing Knowledge**	Mind, body, spirit/intuition, reflection, emotions, relationships as important aspects and conduits of knowledge
Compartmentalized and separate; belief that understanding how the parts work separately, abstractly, and in isolation will lead to the greatest understanding	**Interconnectedness of What is Being Learned**	Contextualized and connected; belief that understanding how things affect each other within the whole, pragmatically, and within community will facilitate understanding
Learning is a private, individual activity; responsible for one's own learning so that family and others are not burdened	**Responsibility for Learning**	Learning is a collective, shared activity; responsible for one's own and others' learning
Linear, task oriented, can be measured and used, to be on time shows respect	**Time**	Circular, seasonal, process oriented, dependent on relationships, to allow for enough time shows respect
Provider and Evaluator of Knowledge—best perspectives and ways of learning, predetermined bounded learning; communication primarily between teacher and students	**Role of the Teacher/ Control**	Facilitator of Learning Experiences— multiple perspectives and ways of learning, emergent constructivist; wide variety of interactions among students and between teacher and students
Others' perspectives are optional for learning. Primarily rely on verbal messages; individuals are paramount, predominantly verbal in both written and oral communications	**Student Interactions**	Others' perspectives and interpretations are important, even essential to learning. High use of nonverbals; collective as paramount, multiple streams of communication
Learn by mastering abstract theory first, followed by testing. Unlikely to include application, experience, or doing in real life	**Sequencing**	Learn by doing, listening to others' experiences, imagining or experiencing first, then drawing out abstract theory

Note. Chávez, Ke, & Herrera (2009). The earliest version of this model was presented in a paper at the 2009 ASHE Conference. This model is developed from a later version of the model in Ke & Chávez (2013).

examples for them to consider. After a thorough exploration of applications of an idea or a process, students who use an integrated perspective will be much more capable of generating or comprehending a theoretical perspective to explain the information they have learned. A typical faculty member approaches the process from the opposite direction, giving theory first and generating examples to illustrate theory. In this situation, as in many similar situations, the person with the greatest power is entitled to frame the standards of performance and is generally unaware that the standards are shaped by culture. People who have less power in this situation—the students—have no choice but to realize that there are at least two approaches and that the one that comes naturally to them is not preferred. As the student bodies of all of our colleges and universities become more diverse, the improvement of teaching and learning requires that faculty members understand that we have been operating in our Western fishbowl and that we are obligated to take a look at the perspective that the fishbowl creates so that we can get outside and critique its utility in educational situations.

Pause for Reflection

Try making a chart for yourself about the typical approaches you take to teaching.

- Do you lecture, standing in front of the students with all of them facing you and not each other?
- Do you believe that each student working alone provides you with the best evidence of student achievement?
- Do you teach theory first and illustrate with examples or vice versa?
- Have you noticed which students respond most effectively to your approach?
- Do you think students who work with others and need reassurance about their perspectives are weaker than those who work alone?
- Do you ask students if they have seen examples of what they are learning in their own world?
- Do you provoke students into thinking about why they are learning the material and whether or not it matters to them?
- Do you ever share any elements of your personal life or concerns with your students?

The Story of Your Discipline or Area of Expertise

Pause for Reflection:
Turning the Culture Lens on Your Own Teaching/
Learning Process

- Do you know the history of your own discipline or area of expertise?

  - When did it start?
  - Who were its creators?
  - How has it changed in relation to cultural developments?
  - What are its fundamental assumptions about what's worth knowing, what knowledge is reliable, and how to help people learn about it?

Disciplines are not static phenomena. They represent ways to organize what is known in the field and then how to expand that knowledge using methods that are considered reliable (Herman, 2013; Kuhn, 1996). Your discipline or area of expertise developed within the Narrative of Higher Education. It reflects the epistemology of the subject/object split, contains assumptions about valid knowledge and the legitimate methods for creating that knowledge, and probably implies approaches to pedagogy. Your discipline also reflects an evolving process of development that occurred as knowledge in related fields evolved and the various research methodologies became more sophisticated. Philosophy was the original mother of all inquiry and understanding until it gave birth to psychology, sociology, and a whole range of other approaches to studying the human condition.

In the past half century, as research became infinitely more sophisticated, disciplines split to very narrow areas of focus and then combined to reflect increasing complexity. Biopsychoneuroimmunology is one such field. It is the study of the interactions among gross (large) biological systems, mental processes or interpretive thought systems, nerve systems, and the combined effects of all of this interaction on the immune system. There really is no such thing as physics (in general) or biology or sociology (in general) anymore with the possible exception of introductory courses.

Integrated Inquiry and Deep Learning

Institutional processes reflect the Western Grand Narrative and have significant implications for the variety of "community engagement" and leadership development efforts that have received much attention recently. If we teach students about leadership in the traditional way, without letting experience precede theory, we will probably be less effective with students from integrated cultures who hope to become leaders in their communities (Burgos, 2013; Stookey, 2012). One student in the Burgos study defined *leadership* as "someone who has their moral strengths and stand up and do what is right. . . . A leader will try to do their best and think about others and go beyond themselves. . . . I associate it with being a role model and leading by example" (p. 29). Clearly this is a contextual approach to learning about leadership expressed by students who were trying to become leaders in their own communities. They did not think about leaders as people who knew a lot before they tried to create change. One of Stookey's students in a business class also commented on the value of an integrated, relational approach to learning: "Giving us a chance to teach these younger students worked out in having all that information sink in for me who new [*sic*] nothing about what we learn" (p. 159).

So-called diversity training presents another challenge to our traditional ways of teaching. Effective diversity training requires that students learn about cultures different from their own, including both the historical and political development of those cultures, and that they be personally aware of the fear, confusion, and feelings of incompetence that may occur when engaging with people from those cultures. From a disciplinary perspective this involves knowledge of anthropology, history, political science, psychology, and interpersonal communication. From an experiential perspective it involves learning to be aware of fear, learning to manage fear, learning to speak respectfully to others whose norms of communication may be unfamiliar to the learner, learning to listen without judgment, and so forth. Knowing about different cultures, particularly in the absence of self-awareness, often leads to the formation of particularly offensive stereotypes based on the idea that one person knows something about another person whether or not the second person believes that this information is an accurate representation of who she or he is. Students from relatively segregated communities (which so many of our communities have become) who are coming to culturally diverse campuses are often exposed to diversity training during orientation. In the absence of knowledge about learning processes and the effects of stress on learning, these students can be reluctant to engage in serious conversations about race for fear of being considered rude. They may retain this attitude in subsequent conversations, adding to the confusion and mistrust that will probably occur. This problem also occurs in the kind of sexual assault training that new students often receive. The purpose of this training is generally to help students learn how to communicate about their sexual interest in each other. Unfortunately, the training is typically presented in an atmosphere of high anxiety, active hormones, and probably a lot of alcohol. Students do not learn well under these conditions and are unlikely to be able to use the skills when they need them in real-life situations. As a result, the training is often ineffective. Think back to your first year in college or your first time away from home. Would training methods that did not engage you directly in conversation about your feelings and reactions to high-anxiety situations such as racial conversation and sexual interaction have helped you adjust, or would you have simply sat through the presentations counting the moments until you could leave? Being exposed to these topics in situations that do not build trust or encourage you to process your feelings generally inhibits understanding and makes using these skills when they are needed very difficult. Under the influence of anxiety, alcohol, or both, would you have remembered what you "learned"? (Effective approaches to helping students learn to communicate with people from different cultures is discussed further in chapter 7.)

Do Students Care? Exchanging Fishbowls and Supporting Deep Learning

Making Student Life Concerns Part of Your Teaching

- What if you spent your first class asking students what they wanted to learn instead of telling them what was on the syllabus?
- What if you told your students why you decided to study in your field and what about it interests you?
- What if you asked your students to discuss the various aspects of their lives that your subject influences and then perhaps to write about how it might affect them in the next 10 years— both personally and globally?
- What if you loosened your commitment to "covering the material" and asked yourself what students need to know about the material?
- What if you never used another bubble sheet but invented student projects that were a major part of assessing learning?

You are the expert on your own field of study and practice, but in the context of your college or university, student requirements about study in your area are often established by curriculum committees and general education requirements. That means you have students in your classes who are just getting your subject "out of the way," so that they can get on to their major. Often they don't care to learn what you have to teach because they don't see the relevance to their own lives or they don't have the skills to be successful. How do you think about that problem? Do you care? For students to appreciate the elegance and utility that you probably see and understand in your discipline, you must share your perspective and then invite students to take the information into their own worlds of meaning. Deep learning occurs when students resonate with the overall context in which ideas and knowledge are offered, because they feel the desire to learn when they resonate with the environment (Chávez & Longerbeam, 2016). Deep learning allows students to understand their own worldview, see its effects on new information, and experiment with alternate perspectives. This skill also allows them to understand perspectives expressed by others and become willing to expand their sense of the value of new or different ideas. Thus, they feel acknowledged in the learning process and are able to listen respectfully to differences of opinion.

What do we know about what students care about today? In general, students care about getting jobs when they graduate, having fun, meeting family responsibilities if they have them, paying off their school loans, living in the global community, participating in community service and internship opportunities, and participating in the enormous range of social networks that shape their worlds. What do employers want students to know and be able to do? They expect flexibility; the ability to collaborate; deep knowledge of the field that supports the work they do and broad knowledge of context; as well as the ability to integrate knowledge from different disciplines, apply knowledge, and see patterns (Kuh, 2011). Does the way you organize and present your courses reflect an awareness of what students think they need to know or what future employers expect them to be able to do? Would a different fishbowl or organization of ideas be more effective in grabbing the attention of these students? Are your students living in the same fishbowl that you live in? Are you interested in exposing the many fishbowls present in your class and inviting students to visit each other in their own "native" environments?

Bridging Your Learning to Your Students' Lives

- What originally drew you to the study of your discipline? Why did it interest you?
- Were there any elements of your personal life that affected any elements of your professional life, particularly marriage or the birth or death of loved ones?
- How much do you care about helping students to learn about your discipline and absorb your fascination with it?
- Does your discipline relate in any way to your sense of who you are and what you care about in the world?

Note

1. For an extensive discussion of switching perspectives, see *Horton Hears a Who!* (Dr. Seuss, 1954).

3

EVERYBODY LEARNS, SOME TEACH

"Pooh," said Rabbit kindly, "you haven't any brain." "I know," said Pooh humbly. Pooh knew what he meant, but being a Bear of Very Little Brain, couldn't think of the words.
(Sibley, 1986, p. 5)

What do you mean when you say, "Learn"? What do you mean when you say, "Teach"? Have you ever learned anything that nobody taught you? Of course you have. How did you learn how to walk? To ride a bike? To be intimate with another person? To avoid your parents when you knew they were angry? To reframe the truth in order to protect yourself or somebody you care about (also known as lying or Covering Up)? If teaching happens and nobody learns, what do you call that? Take some time to think about these questions before reading further.

Try to recall a moment when you learned something really important that catapulted you to the next stage of taking care of yourself. Humans have only two innate instincts: sucking and fear of falling. Everything else is learned from experience, demonstration, instruction, or trial and error with comments or reflections. We learn to be humans living in families and communities. Most of what we learn is not "taught" in any conventional sense. Do you remember learning to tie your shoes, brush your teeth, or braid your hair? Do you remember the moment you figured it out? Before that moment somebody else was doing it for you or showing you and suddenly you could do it yourself.

Perhaps you learned that braiding could be done alone but it typically looked better if somebody else did it for you; that is, learned about collaboration and support in addition to hair braiding.

> Try to recall a moment when you learned something really important that catapulted you to the next stage of taking care of yourself.

Now move further into your adult life. What are some of the most important things you have learned as an adult, particularly things that involve behavioral skills and emotional self-management? Survey areas of your life where you have had to learn new skills and conceptualizations in order to improve your work and relationships to be successful.

Learning, Reflection, and Experience

Unexpected Learning

- What did you learn?
- Write down the physical skills, your age, your emotional reaction, the place it happened, other people who were with you, time of the year, and anything else that you can recall.

Reflection in Present Time

- How do you feel as you reflect on that exciting moment?
- Did your life change as a result of what you learned?
- Were you proud of yourself?
- Are you having trouble right now getting back to that moment because it seems silly or childish?
- Take a moment to experience all the feelings that emerge in this exercise.
- Can you describe your own learning process when you are faced with an unfamiliar situation and you learn how to deal with it to your own satisfaction?

There are many ways to describe this kind of complex learning, which involves so many dimensions including these four: knowledge acquisition, skill development, emotional engagement, and meaning making (Fried, 2012). *Engaged learning* (Caine, Caine, McClintic, & Klimek, 2005) is designed to help students acquire knowledge, apply it, and place it in their own system of meaning making. This approach suggests that effective learning must involve acknowledgment of brain physiology, appropriate levels of stress for goal achievement and motivation, integration of new information with biographical experience, and active reflection by the student about the information and the contexts in which it might be used. *Transformative learning* (Mezirow & Associates, 2000) adds another dimension, the critical analysis of previously held structures of meaning and the expansion of ideas about the significance of new information in a variety of contexts. We rarely learn isolated facts. Knowledge that is retained is almost always part of a larger structure of significance—we learn what we need to know, typically in order to accomplish something or to understand something we care about.

Life skills constitute a very large part of what we need to know. Every time we make an embarrassing mistake, if we are reflective, we make an effort to learn something so we don't repeat the error. This kind of learning is closely related to human development. There is a controversy in the student development literature (Keeling, 2008) about the appropriate terms to describe the acquisition of life skills. Is this process of improving one's ability to manage emotions *hardwired* into brain function so that epigenetic development occurs organically? Or is the process of learning adult life skills best described from a *transformative learning* perspective that involves experiment, reflection, action, and evolution of perspective and skill (Kegan, 1994; Mezirow & Associates, 2000)? It is the assertion of this book that the answer is "both." Human beings learn their way through life by engaging with the environment and the challenges it presents. We then invent coping methods to manage these challenges with or without the assistance of other people. Life skill development is a learning process that is supported by brain development. In much the same way as we learn to drive or play a sport, people learn certain day-to-day physical skills, train the body/mind to use those skills, and practice the skills until they become more or less automatic. Then we imagine the "perfect" use of the skill, such as a golf swing or a basketball shot, and we feed the knowledge generated by our imagination and observation back into our physical learning process. The brain accommodates these demands and insights so that the body performs the skills. The conscious mind observes the use of the skills in action and creates modifications to improve the skills. This is a completely integrated process. Polanyi (1966) called this feedback process *tacit learning*. The knower and that which is to be known become a unified phenomenon consisting of interaction between subject and object. Subsequent brain research has documented Polanyi's assertions. It is impossible to separate cognition from affect, or the knower from the known, in any human learning experience.

> Life skill development is a learning process that is supported by brain development.

Learning in Your Discipline or Area of Expertise

Every field has its own paradigm for learning, conducting research, and presenting new knowledge to other scholars. The learning/research paradigm for each discipline tends to be rigid and resistant to change (Kuhn, 1996). Nevertheless, our understanding of the world in which we live changes when paradigms are disrupted, despite the discomfort that this process tends to cause. Einstein is reported to have commented on this phenomenon many times, stating, "Anyone who has never made a mistake has never tried anything new. . . . Great spirits have always encountered violent opposition from mediocre minds. . . . Learn from yesterday, live for today, hope for tomorrow. The important thing is not to stop questioning" ("Albert Einstein Quotes," n.d.). He was not patient with people who couldn't reconsider their own ideas. As a scholar you probably arrived at some point in your own career when you questioned the dominant paradigm in your field and began to wonder about challenging the reigning authorities. The more divergent the new ideas are from the old orthodoxy, the more uncomfortable the process. Whatever you learned by considering new ideas also included what you learned about the consequences of challenging the established truth.

Teaching the Way People Learn

> ### Reflection on Your Own Learning
>
> - Remember one time in your own academic career when you learned something that disoriented your previous frame of reference.
> - Did the shift in perspective also result in a shift in feelings or behavior?
> - Did you begin challenging other ideas in the field?
> - Did your new approach disrupt relationships?
> - What you learned wasn't just an "add-on." This new framework probably rippled into the rest of your life.

The reality of integrated learning calls into question most of the pedagogy used in higher education. Students may, and it is hoped will, learn content in any area they study. Simultaneously, they learn the skills of listening, note taking, observing, preparing, managing their time, cooperating with other students, and so forth. In laboratory or fieldwork courses there are also numerous manual and behavioral skills to be learned. Whatever students learn in one domain has the potential to ripple into other domains of their lives and either confirm what they thought they knew or cause them to question apparent truths.

Let's take introductory social science courses as examples. Students may begin to learn about the powerful effects of social class structure on opportunities for people who grow up in poverty. In a psychology class students may see pictures of the developing brains of two small children, one in a family with sufficient resources to buy good food, toys, and excellent day care and one in a family that can afford to buy only lower grade food, has no money for stimulating toys, and has little money for day care. They will see that the child with fewer resources has a significantly slower process of brain development. Students may learn about residential segregation and its effects on the quality of neighborhood schools. What would constitute meaningful learning in any of these courses—or effective teaching? Is it sufficient for a professor to present the "facts" and ask students to be able to discuss them, or is there a personal dimension that would make this learning meaningful for students? Is it appropriate to insert a discussion of ethics or morality into this objectivist description of the consequences of poverty? In a class with students from both "have" and "have-not" backgrounds, how would the conversation be managed so that different perspectives can be expressed and different emotional responses acknowledged? Is objectivity an appropriate approach to the complete learning process or is there more? What do you mean when you say Learning? What do you want your students to learn? Facts are essential—what is the role of the faculty at the border of facts, consequences, and personal meaning?

> Take a moment to identify two or three topics that typically come up in your courses and often generate differences of opinion. If you wanted students to learn about different perspectives on these topics, how would your teaching style be affected?

The Personal and the Impersonal: Is This a Binary or an Iterative Process?

Student development is a term widely used in the student affairs profession but not often included in academic discourse. Student development occurs throughout a student's life in college. Students are learning to develop in all areas of their college life, and new information is constantly integrated into the developmental learning process. Some developmental areas in which emerging adult students engage are identity formation, vocation selection, faith and values development, and community/civic engagement. The campus may be administered in silos, but the student who learns about the effect of nutrition on brain development or the effects of socioeconomic status on the quality of neighborhood schools has the potential to integrate this learning. And that student, unconsciously and consciously, is reflecting on the meaning of all of it whether it is discussed in class or not. Many students may decide that what they learn in class is just an exercise in memorization with no personal consequences. If nobody has taken the time to help them move through a reflective review of the facts and frameworks, everyone involved will have completed a very expensive charade at the end of every semester. What do you want your students to learn?

> Do you want your students to learn to reflect on the subject matter you teach, or just to remember it until the test is over?

Learning to Be a Contributing Member of Family and Community

In the domain of student life students are also faced with incongruent facts and experiences. What confusion might a student face when learning that the word *Islam* means peace; that most Moslem women students who cover themselves do not feel oppressed; that Israel and Hamas are bombing each other and newscasters are referring to the conflict in religious, not political terms; or that Moslems generally observe the same dietary restrictions as orthodox Jews? What might happen when a White student from North America shares a room with a student from Nigeria whose grades are far higher and who studies harder and does not drink? What might happen when two students (or 10) get into a conversation about the role of family in their lives? Some students affirm that family is the most important part of their lives and they will never move more than five miles from home, whereas others can't wait to leave their families and express genuine dislike for their parents. In all these cases, students would be able to negotiate these experiences far more effectively if they could apply what they are learning in their courses to their lives with fellow students.

Almost every college in the United States includes in its mission statement something about character development and the creation of an informed citizenry. This purpose is part of the narrative, or story, of higher education in the United States. The difficulty with this aspect of mission statements is that current pedagogy and epistemology exclude inquiry into personal meaning from academic study. The reality is that very few departments in our colleges have a sense of responsibility for supporting student development in this way. Student organizations help students learn leadership in very practical ways, but students rarely receive credit for this learning and there is rarely an academic component to the learning process. Students learn community engagement from service projects and service learning requirements, but there is generally no systematic way to plan or assess learning in these activities. Students are frequently exposed to "diversity training," which is training with a focus on awareness of feelings and suggested changes in student attitudes and behavior (e.g., racism, sexism, homophobia, religious prejudice, ableism, etc.). There is typically very little presentation of information related to any of these issues from contextual, historic, or disciplinary perspectives. If learning goals or assessment of learning outcomes are part of the training process, they generally do not ask students about increases in their knowledge of context, history, or disciplinary analysis or attempt to connect new information to behavior or attitude changes. Students in social service and teaching majors almost always have to complete internships. These courses come closest to integrating theoretical and experiential learning with the expectation of helping students integrate their learning into their personal narrative. Faith-based institutions focus heavily on character development within the faith system; however, the doctrine of separation of church and state presents a considerable roadblock to discussion of character development in public institutions. This conversation is typically relegated to student affairs offices, counseling, and conversations with clergy who are not officially part of the institution. Humanities students study artistic and literary presentations of complex human beings. This is the most likely place for character development to be considered, even if it is once removed.

Pedagogical Conundra and Personal Reflection

A *pedagogical conundrum* is a fancy way of saying, "This problem is confusing, frustrating, and doesn't seem to have a workable resolution." In response to all this information about student development, you may be thinking, "I am a [fill in the blank; for example, physicist, sociologist, professor of literature, mathematician], and nobody ever told me that any of this was my responsibility. I have no training and little interest in community engagement or character development. I have no time for these kinds of relationships with students. I have too many students. I have my own research. Don't they do this on their own time?" If you really want to take this line of thinking to the extreme, you could consider your other significant relationships such as those with your spouse, your children, and your family of origin. You might want to ask yourself if the way you handle those relationships has anything to do with the way you manage your relationships with students, colleagues, or other staff. If you're good at relationships with family, you probably will be good at relating to students, although you may not immediately see the connection. The reverse is also true. It's all about skill development and emotional self-management.

So we return to the initial question: What do you mean when you use the term *learn*? What do you do and expect to accomplish when you teach? If teaching occurs and only facts are learned and forgotten shortly after the completion of the course, are you satisfied with the effort you have expended in "teaching"? If you are a professor, do you care about student character development and the students' ability to articulate and discuss their emerging value systems in this fast-changing and very confusing and frightening world? If you are a member of the student affairs profession, do you ever think about the benefits that would accrue to student learning if students could connect what they learn in class to their lives outside class? What do you think the consequences would be if you started talking about learning and development or behavior across faculty/student affairs lines?

What's the Point?

Because of current research on learning and brain function, we now know that all learning that is retained is integrated. Nevertheless, we continue to organize our institutions in silos and give credit only for "academic" learning, which typically means fact recall and problem solving in the disciplines. We generally do not acknowledge the complete learning process and often treat social/emotional learning as "fluff." Traditional academic approaches to teaching do not incorporate what we know about learning, and, therefore, much of what is learned tends to disappear over time. What is learned in the student life domain tends to be retained but not enhanced by all of the relevant academic knowledge that is potentially available. The point is that learning could be much more powerful, sustainable, and useful if all educators looked at their silos and moved out of them for conversations about learning. Einstein would be very pleased.

4

ENTR'ACTE

Is "Teach" a Transitive Verb?

There is no such thing as a neutral educational process. Education either functions as an instrument which is used to facilitate the integration of the younger generation into the logic of the present system and bring about conformity to it, or it becomes the practice of freedom.
(Sharll, 1990, p. 15)

W hat do you mean when you say, "Teach"? The structure of the English language (subject/verb/object) assumes that an agent acts on an object. It assumes action by a subject on an external object and does not automatically imply interaction. With language modifications, interactions can obviously be described. Languages that rely on verbal gerunds, or process words, to a greater degree than English does have a much easier time describing interactions. There seems to be a very strong correlation between cultural context and language structure. For example, "Confucian ethics emphasized the indivicual's connectedness with the natural world and other people. . . . Personal fulfillment could only be attained by establishing harmonious relationships with the physical and social environment. The Japanese worldview—based on Confucianism—emphasizes interdependence" (Fogel, Stevenson, & Messenger, 1996, p. 36). In contrast, the United States and most other cultures in the Judeo-Christian tradition emphasize "self-knowledge and personal responsibility. Personal fulfillment and self-reliance [are] prerequisites for contributing to the common good. . . . The United States' worldview emphasizes the autonomous individual" (Fogel et al., 1996, p. 36). Childrearing practices and cultural value systems vary according to these fundamental assumptions. Americans consider dependence to be a temporary state and work very hard to help children learn to make decisions and become more autonomous. Japanese people, in contrast, teach children to depend first on their mothers and then on the family and community. Independence is not considered a socially valued personality trait (Fogel et al., 1996). Honoring connections and creating harmony are highly esteemed virtues.

Independence and autonomy imply separation. This notion of separation of subject from object, people from their environment, and people from each other is part of the cultural narrative of the United States and higher education in this country. What most of us don't realize is that this approach is a construct, not The Way Things Are. In fact, there is currently a great deal of evidence (Bohm, 2003; Eisenstein, 2013; Laszlo, 2006; Wheatley, 1999) that this narrative is The Way Things Aren't. All civilizations have had what Bohm (1985) calls "general notions of cosmic order, and of the nature of reality as a whole" (back cover). Our perspective, our fishbowl, hypothesizes separation and doesn't realize that this perspective is a hypothesis.

What's the Point?

The point is that the current idea of The Way Things Are and the language we speak profoundly influence the way we think about teaching, learning, and other people, including students. We can't help but think of teaching as an activity in which we engage as subjects, by transmitting our version of reliable knowledge to students/objects. In this case they are objects of the preposition *to*. Do we teach students, subject matter, or learning process? We teach about subject matter. By creating learning environments, typically lecturing, we demonstrate learning processes or at least thinking processes. Do we ever teach subject matter? Linguistically this is a reasonable sentence, but empirically teaching implies learning, so how would we teach subject matter? We teach students about subject matter. Here are a couple of typical sentences that make linguistic sense, but not empirical sense: "I'm going to get my education." Is education an object? "When I graduate college . . ."

Grammatically that one is incorrect, but structurally it means that I will do something to college called "graduating." In our personal lives, "I dumped him/her." It's a metaphor but it implies an agent acting on an object, not a relationship ending. It should be obvious by now that I was an English literature major and have been an English teacher with 12-year-olds. It's a very difficult process. You can help them learn about themselves through the study of literature, but teaching them about grammar, for which they see no purpose, is a much harder task.

The point is that students are never objects. They are always subjects. They are always learning something, and learning is not limited to verbal exchanges or the ability to rewrite what has been heard or seen. When students sit in classrooms, with or without various Internet-connected devices, they are learning behaviorally, emotionally, and cognitively. They have learned what time of day is the best or most feasible to take classes; who the good professors are; how many things they can do at once with their devices while appearing to listen; whom to sit next to; and whether or not the notes will be posted online, making class attendance unnecessary. They are also probably thinking about whether the class they are sitting in has anything to do with the rest of their lives or anything they care about. They are planning their weekend, their work schedule, and the best way to connect with their friends or potential partners.

Students, Learning, and Development

The purpose of organisms is to organize and what human beings organize is meaning. Meaning making is the activity of composing a sense of the connection among things: a sense of pattern, order, form and significance. To be human is to seek coherence and correspondence. . . . Patterning, testing and recomposing activity occurs in every aspect of human life and manifests itself in meaning. (Parks, 2000, p. 19)

Students are always people in transition regardless of their age. Traditionally students go to college at age 18, the time in the dominant culture when young people are expected to become significantly more autonomous even if they don't physically stop living with their families. However, we must consider the wide variety of today's students. Think about veterans returning to college, or attending for the first time, are in transition from military to civilian life. Displaced workers are hoping to learn whatever they need for new careers. People whose children or spouses have left them go to college to try to make sense out of their new life status. In American society, people go to college as a means of helping themselves Figure Things Out—either what things mean or what to do about the things that have disrupted their lives.

The reality, more formally stated, is that students are attempting to shape and envision their place in their emerging world, and they cannot do it alone or simply by ingesting new information without contextual frameworks. In Freirian terms (Freire, 1990) they are attempting to name the world and their relationship to it in a process of dialogue. They are learning what Freire calls *praxis*, a process of reflecting on the world in order to determine ways to maximize freedom and then take action to achieve their goals. Mezirow and associates (2000) call this *transformative learning*, a process by which people realize that they are seeing the world through a particular frame of reference that is not universal. They then learn to critique their own perspective and attempt to understand the perspectives of others, also through dialogue. In Parks's (2000) terms, they are creating or observing new patterns of meaning.

A fairly sophisticated level of cognitive development is necessary for students to be able to reflect on their own current meaning-making systems and then ask themselves if those systems are still working for them (Kegan, 2000). As a professor are you trying to integrate your students into the logic of the current system so that they can conform to it, or are you trying to introduce them to the greater freedom of critical thinking and challenging their own unacknowledged narrative (Shaull, 1990)? Are you using your teaching opportunities to help students learn this process? In your classroom are students subjects or objects? Do they learn facts (only) or are they putting those facts into a broader context of meaning and value? Now we're going down the rabbit hole.

Let's consider learning as a process that includes and, it is hoped, benefits from teaching. What do you hope your students will learn from you—about your discipline and about the reasons why you think it's important? Can you separate one from the other? If teaching is not a transitive verb and students are not objects, how does that change the way we engage in the learning process?

Take a break. You probably need it. I certainly do.

5

SELF-AUTHORSHIP

A New Narrative of Learning

When I grow up I'll write a book about me—but I'm grown up now. At least there's no room to grow up any more here. . . . Shall I never get any older than I am now? That would be a comfort in one way—I'll never be an old woman—but then—there'll always be lessons to learn! Oh, I shouldn't like that. (Carroll, 1865/1993, p. 21)

The classic model of teaching and learning implies information transfer in a relatively "objective" or fact-based manner. Information to be transferred or learned is presumably separate from the learner and the teacher, is empirical (verifiable by experience or experiment), is impersonal, and is shaped only by the context that is directly connected to the knowledge. For example, water exists in different states depending on the presence of heat, but not depending on the attitude of the observer. The state of the knower, as influenced by either a narrative of meaning or a particular emotional state at the time when learning occurs, is presumably irrelevant. Even if you are upset when water changes from liquid to gas at 212°F, the fact is that 212°F/100°C is the boiling point of water. Or even if you believe that the finger of God is responsible for raising the temperature of water, the boiling point remains the same. The authority that validates the knowledge to be learned may be embodied in a professor or in a wider domain of experts, but it is rarely embodied in the students. Students are not considered authorities, and in general their opinions about valid and reliable knowledge in any particular discipline are considered less significant than those of widely accepted persons of authority.

How do we think about authority and its sources? *Authority, authorship, author,* and *authenticity* all have the same linguistic root, *auctor* (Latin), which means originator. The derivative Latin word *auctoritas* also signifies power, opinion, and decision maker. What is *self-authorship?* One way to describe this process is the ability to write and originate the story of one's own life, one's personal narrative. Alice had clearly lost control of the process when she fell down the Rabbit Hole. Losing control of the story of one's self is a Profoundly Disorienting experience. Has anybody ever said to you, "You're not that kind of person," and then you began to wonder what kind of person the other person thought you were? Who's in charge of deciding Who You Are? In this situation the opinions of the individual about his or her own life experiences take precedence over the opinions of all others even though the opinions of others are not necessarily to be discounted. Baxter Magolda and King (2004) describe the "shift from authority dependence to self-authorship which (occurs) by challenging learners to see the composing of reality in complex terms and supporting them in coordinating their beliefs, values and interpersonal loyalties" (p. xix). Once a person begins to believe that she can be her own author, this shift has begun.

Belenky, Clinchy, Goldberger, and Tarule (1986) documented this process in *Women's Ways of Knowing*. The authors used different language for the same process, as their subjects moved from relying totally on outside sources for decision making to framing their world and their place in it as an integrated process of articulation, reflection, action, and transformation. *Transformative learning* also describes this type of change. Students realize that they have a frame of reference, or narrative about events, but that they are not defined by their frame of reference, which was presumably given to them by an external authority (Kegan, 2000). They have a frame of reference that they can observe, contemplate, compare to others, and change if evidence suggests that it is inadequate for understanding something. "One goes from being psychologically 'written by' the socializing process to 'writing upon it,' a shift from a socialized to a self-authorizing process" (p. 59).

A Student Story

Once I was teaching a sophomore honors course on the history of education. Several times I asked the students what they thought about a particular issue. Silence. I became very frustrated with their apparent unwillingness to participate in a discussion so I stopped my lecture and asked a process question: "What's going on here? You all have plenty to say outside of class. Why so quiet in class?" The jaw-dropping response from one student: "Nobody ever asked me about my opinion before." In an honors course from a student who had graduated from an "excellent" high school. No self-authorizing going on there.

Self-authorizing is also called *growing up* and learning to create and support your own opinions/critical thinking. It is one element of human development in which cognitive processes (increased complexity of thought, ability to think conceptually and compare systems of meaning making) are supported by biological processes (brain development, increased connections among neurotransmitters). This in itself is the "composing of reality in complex terms." The aforementioned students did not see that school had anything to do with self-authorship and apparently neither did most of their previous teachers. For them school was about learning facts and repeating facts.

Self-authorship, the process of composing a life, your own life, is the most profound task that college students face, regardless of their age, their fields of study, their career choice, or any other future plans (Bateson, 1990). Self-authorship provides the context in which all decisions are made. The widely accepted elements of student development, including identity formation, vocation, sense of purpose, interpersonal competence, and autonomy/interdependence (Chickering & Reisser, 1993), all provide elements of the larger personal narrative that addresses such questions as: Who am I and what do I have to offer? What is my place in the world and what kind of a life do I want? These questions preoccupy students regardless of field of study. Students from non-Eurocentric cultures experience the questions differently. In non-Eurocentric cultures where roles are typically assigned, students may worry about how they will fulfill the responsibilities expected by their communities. Among students from Eurocentric backgrounds, the struggle more likely will be to address the issue of defining roles: What does each person have to offer? In both situations, students are likely to struggle with these issues because college transforms and illuminates all their assumptions about life's possibilities. Academic study is one way to address these questions, but it is not the only way to do so. Unfortunately, because of the way that most universities are organized and the ways that most academicians have been trained, questions of personal meaning are generally not addressed in most courses, particularly large lecture courses.

Self-authorship, the process of composing a life, your own life, is the most profound task that college students face, regardless of their age, their fields of study, their career choice, or any other future plans (Bateson, 1990).

The Cartesian Split and the Twenty-First-Century Connection

Descartes believed that "the essence of mind is to think and the essence of matter is to exist—and the two never meet" (as cited in Herman, 2013, p. 345). He described human beings as "spiders at the center of an enormous web, not of our own making . . . [or] ghosts in the machine" (p. 345). This perspective, which gave rise to our ability to observe nature and the physical world from a removed and presumably "objective" perspective, also engendered the creation of the scientific method and most standard research methods in the physical and social sciences. The impact of Descartes's insight and formulation cannot be overstated or overvalued. Without it the Industrial Revolution might not have occurred. We probably would not have flown into space or radically diminished the number of diseases worldwide. However, the Cartesian worldview does not account for all the phenomena of human experience, and sometimes it is quite misleading or destructive.

One of the areas in which Cartesian assumptions are not helpful is understanding how people make sense of their lives and how they integrate new knowledge into their personal and cultural narratives. When students learn decontextualized facts without the opportunity to contemplate the implications of those facts for their lives and the lives of others, the consequences are often less than positive.

Another Student Story

Once upon a time I was interviewing applicants for my graduate program in student affairs. Students were asked to comment on differential rates of academic success among various ethnic and racial groups. That is, why do Euro- and Asian American students succeed in school at higher rates than African American or Latino stsudents, even when family income and education levels are held constant? One White student who participated in an interview with several students of color had taken a "cultural diversity" course as an undergrad. He proceeded to explain the generalities he had learned about the various groups he had studied and moved from his knowledge to his ability to generalize about members of these groups. Three other applicants were students of color, who tried to keep their faces from revealing their emotions as they listened to his opinion. It was obvious that they were offended and felt disrespected. He had never stopped to consider his own membership in the Euro-American group or the effect of his comments on members of other groups. He knew a lot of facts. But he had no idea how they played out in an interpersonal situation, nor did he realize the broader consequences of his mode of expression.

The student in this story had not been exposed to the notion of co-constructing knowledge, at least in this domain. He had learned the data from texts and presumably from lectures, but he had not taken time to consider the consequences of this information in his daily life and interactions with others. Co-constructing knowledge is a process that contradicts the Cartesian notion of the subject/object split and is relatively unusual in college pedagogy. Co-construction is based on the belief that knowledge does not exist absolutely. Knowledge is created in dialogue among the knowers about the phenomena under discussion and what they mean to the participants. Knowledge can be created or apprehended only by knowers and all knowers have a slightly different understanding of what is known.

Plato's idea of the Forms is a key source of the notion that knowledge is absolute and can be apprehended but not influenced by the people who know. From a biological perspective this belief system can be easily challenged. Absolute knowledge may exist, but the only way that people have of apprehending it, or learning, is through their perceptual and interpretive apparatus—their eyes, ears, and other senses including extensions of these such as telescopes, microscopes, and other instruments. The only way knowers have of making sense out of the known is through their own interpretive processes, which are (for our purposes) based in each brain. Every person's brain is slightly different from all other brains and every person's life experience, which has both shaped the brain and influenced its contents, is also different. So observers and inquirers can come to a consensual definition of *reality* in any given situation, but there is no absolute way of agreeing on all the details of the phenomenon. Simply put, it just isn't possible for one person to know the whole story of everything. In fact, the whole the following may never be known or may be evolving. Vygotsky, one of the earliest theoreticians of learning and development, developed the following fundamental premises for learning: (a) children construct knowledge, (b) learning can lead to development, (c) development cannot be separated from its social context, and (d) language plays a central role in mental development. These ideas are all interconnected and built upon each other. Vygotsky's basic premise was that children make sense out of their experiences, both with objects and with other people, by labeling, creating categories of understanding, and discussing what they think is going on in their world. Meaning making, at least for children, requires a social context to occur. As children master language and create more comprehensive categories of understanding (Vygotsky, 1994), they become more capable of reflection.

Self-Authorship and the Construction of Knowledge

When You Teach . . . What Do Your Students Learn?

- When your students learn about the history of immigration laws, do you ever wonder how their ethnic background and time of family immigration affects their understanding?
- Have you ever wondered why courses in African American studies are mostly taken by African American students? Or women's studies courses by women?

- If you teach about Middle Eastern politics, do you ever wonder if Anglo-Americans, Jewish Americans, and Americans whose families come from the Middle East learn the same things? Interpret events the same way? Do your students learn to talk to each other or fight with each other?
- If you teach mathematics, do you ever discuss the ethnic backgrounds of the great thinkers in this field? Do you think it matters? How many great mathematicians come from China, from Africa, from India? Would knowing this information affect the success rates of any of your students? Is the truth the same in a binary system as it is in a base 10 system? Is accuracy a more valid criterion than truth?

Our initial questions reemerge: On what basis of authority do students decide what matters to them, what is real, how reliable knowledge is developed, and how they will use what they know? People cannot create knowledge outside the context of who they think they are; what their life experience has taught them; or beyond a whole range of social, political, and economic circumstances that shape their personal narrative and their cultural worldview. In light of what we have learned since Descartes formulated his famous aphorism, it just isn't possible.

The master's degree program that I run is based on a set of ideas about social justice and the role of higher education in the United States in equalizing opportunity for members of oppressed groups. Students learn information on the effects of worldview and cultural frameworks on the behavior and success rates of college students. Students in this program learn about oppression and differential treatment of people based on their disability status, their gender, their sexual orientation, and so forth. They've heard it all before. In some cases they have been treated differently or ignored or harassed based on these characteristics. Many have been trained by their parents either to protect themselves from members of groups who are prejudiced about their group or to ignore differences and pretend that they aren't significant. Everybody knows what to say to be considered politically correct. About four weeks into the semester, I change the subject. The first part of the semester is devoted, among other things, to building trust within the group. Instead of talking *about* these issues in an intellectual way we begin to discuss the ways they have affected students in the class. Students of color describe the ways their high school counselors often discourage them from going to a four-year college or the ways they have been followed by detectives in clothing stores or what the term *driving while Black* means to them. Latino students explain how it feels when they are walking down the street in their own neighborhood and they hear the locks on a car driven by a White person clicking down. Everybody gasps when the White professor calls out White people for being White and acting White and not realizing that they are White. The students of color don't believe it and the White students don't get it. It often Takes Time and Tissues until they do.

The shift from *learning about* to *learning* depends on emotional involvement or caring, description of personal experience, face-to-face dialogue, and a teacher who is willing to self-disclose (appropriately, around issues of the subject under discussion), confront incongruities in student comments, and require that each student listen respectfully to the perspective and experience of every other student. Once students get over the shock and fear of the initial conversations, it isn't so bad. In fact, they get used to it and find the whole process fairly liberating. They are able to befriend students from different backgrounds in an authentic way. They are able to ask questions about differences and are not forced to remain ignorant out of fear of offending somebody. And when they do offend somebody, usually with no malicious intent, they learn how to apologize and that rarely does a person die of embarrassment. Simultaneously they will be more likely to remember facts about the cultural history of other groups and to become more effective employees in diverse work situations because the facts they learn are embedded in emotional responses and not all of the emotions are comfortable. All of this learning occurs because the process is integrated, personal, and authentic. The teaching involves a set of skills that are is not typically in the toolbox of many academic faculty: the ability to confront; a willingness to question students about personal reactions; the ability to ask students to speak directly to each other, not to the professor; the ability to acknowledge emotions and ask students to analyze their own feelings. This set of skills requires additional training for the faculty member or the presence of a trained person, usually a member of the student affairs staff, in the classroom.

Classroom Dialogue

The discussion is about Hair—which is a Big Topic among Black people and a subject of curiosity for White people. The teacher asks Black students to describe some awkward experiences they've had with Whites about Hair. White students are very quiet. The teacher then prompts the White students to explain why they haven't participated in the conversation. One of the students engages in the following dialogue with the teacher:

Teacher: "Why are you so quiet?"
Student: "I don't want to offend anybody."
Teacher: "Have you ever offended anybody at any other time?"
Student: "Of course."
Teacher: "What did you do then?"
Student: "I apologized."
Teacher: "How is this different?"

More Silence. The teacher then says, "Let's talk about what you're feeling, what the Black students are feeling, and why this is such a difficult conversation. If you don't take any risks you'll never learn anything—you'll just keep on knowing what you already know. Is that what you want to do?" (See Appendix A for more suggestions on facilitating discussions.)

Self-Authorship Is Often a Confusing and Painful Process

You can feel self-authorship begin to develop as soon as students realize that they can and must interpret their own experience and respect the experience of others even if they have never had a similar experience. One Black student exclaimed, "I never knew Black people could own houses until my sophomore year in college when I went to a friend's house." The first student grew up in the projects and had never had a Black friend whose family owned a home. Another Black student described seeing the hidden mirrors and cameras in a convenience store above the area that contained cosmetics for people of color. As far as she could tell, there were no similar devices above the section that contained cosmetics for White people. White students have trouble believing this, but they are required to see each person as an authority on his or her own experience. Self-authorship grows.

In every class there are meaningful differences among students that highlight the effect of different narratives on the interpretation of common experiences. Historically, faculty were expected to emphasize the "facts" followed by various perspectives on the facts derived from the comments of authorities. It is not traditional to ask students to develop an opinion about any set of facts based on their personal experience. In fact, that approach is typically discouraged and described as anecdotal. Technically, *anecdotal* means that data were collected nonsystematically. Nonsystematic data collection is not scientific, but that does not necessarily mean that it is invalid. Anecdotal data are considered invalid within the scientific worldview, which is a belief system, a guide to accuracy in the physical universe, but not as significant or valid in other areas of concern. In other belief systems anecdotal evidence is often considered a signpost to greater insight.

One very big problem in permitting students to create opinions based on their anecdotal, personal experience is that there is no way of challenging what they say or finding out "the truth." If one student says she has been consistently told that she should major in math because she is Chinese and she really wants to be an artist, is that evidence of racism or just her personal experience? Do you think our Asian student would get a different response from her counselor if she said, "Just because I am Chinese doesn't mean I am good at math or enjoy it. I want to be an artist. Can you give me some advice about how to proceed?" That would be a comment worthy of a person who was becoming self-authorizing. I have noticed that African American women in my classes frequently speak very well but often do not write very well. They lack technical training in sentence and paragraph structure and organization of arguments. When I ask them if anybody has ever told them they need to learn these skills they look confused and say that some professors tell them they need to write better but nobody has ever told them what that means. My conclusion: Some of these professors can't tell the difference between racism and good writing. They are *afraid* to correct these students, leaving them with a Big Problem that should have been solved early in their academic careers. I infer that we have fear masquerading as cultural sensitivity. I couldn't claim the scientific validity of my experience or of the typical experience of our Asian student. But that does not mean it isn't significant and should be ignored.

What's the Point?

When students have differences of opinion based on conflicting facts or faulty logic, professors are trained to bring more accurate evidence and challenge the logic. When students have been insulted, ignored, or hurt and these powerful emotions come out in class, most professors have no training in what to do about the ensuing distress. As a result, there is generally no manageable way to continue the conversation because a large part of our dominant narrative in higher education is that we should rely on our intellect to enhance our understanding and search for accuracy. There is no place in that narrative that tells us to use our emotions to enhance our understanding, to give credence to a range of emotional reactions, or to incorporate emotions into the domain of understanding what we study. Emotions are a huge part of our disorienting Rabbit Hole. Now that we're down here, whether we want to be or not, what do we do about it?

Research indicates that stress impairs learning; the higher the level of stress, the greater the confusion and memory loss (Begley, 2007). When emotions erupt in a class and both the students and the professor experience stress, very little learning occurs—except learning how to change the subject, dismiss the class, and possibly confirm preexisting prejudices. Another example is that when students are under unmanageable levels of stress prior to an exam they will become more confused and less efficient as learners. Life without stress is not possible, but in the case of prepping for an exam, there are usually student services that teach students how to study, how to organize their thoughts, and how to stay calm during the exam. The professor is not responsible for that part of the process. When an unanticipated eruption of distress occurs in a class because of the subject matter itself, there are generally no comparable support services.

Self-authorship is often disruptive and upsetting. Some aspects of self-authorship are related to students confronting the variation of human experience present among their peers in regard to social, political, economic, and cultural differences. Is it possible to begin to integrate this knowledge into the way we teach about these subjects? Do you believe that self-authorship is a proper function of higher education or that it is part of your role to support students in integrating facts with personal meaning? Is Teaching the Facts about periodic unemployment in capitalist systems; U.S. history; the sociology of neighborhood deterioration; or the relationship among nutrition, mental stimulation, and brain development sufficient? Does Teaching the Facts and leaving students to understand what these insights mean to them personally contribute to their self-authorship? Do you want students who know what they think, are able to explain their opinions, and also describe why they care about whatever issue is under discussion? Or do you want students who say what you think and have little understanding of why they should know this information? If self-authorship is an integrated process of "challenging learners to see the composing of reality in complex terms, and supporting them in coordinating their beliefs, values and interpersonal loyalties" (Baxter Magolda & King, 2004, p. xix), does it make sense for the institution to address this process in separate areas of responsibility? Perhaps it makes more sense to teach all educators about the integrated process and the role of emotions and meaning making in learning so that they can support the development of self-authorship in their students, regardless of where or when the Moment of Insight occurs.

> Do you want your students to know what they think, to be able to explain their opinions, and to describe why they care about whatever issue is under discussion? Or do you want students who say what you think and have little understanding of why they should know this information?

My Moment of Insight

Once upon a time—actually three different times—I took statistics courses. One text had a sombrero on the front cover. It was a good text and I kept it. Periodically I looked at the sombrero and wondered why this picture was chosen for the front of a statistics book. Sometime in my mid-40s it hit me. That sombrero was a three-dimensional representation of a normal distribution curve. By that point I had learned to read and understand statistical descriptions in various research articles, and I knew it was all about relationships among phenomena as described in numerical and formulaic terms. I understood relationships—cause and effect as well as correlative and interpersonal. But I never understood that sombrero until I knew it was about relationships. Making a connection that made personal sense to me finally allowed me to understand my sombrero.

A More Serious Insight

One of my friends has often wondered why Jewish families "devour their young," in his words. He is Jewish and so am I. I have often observed the particular kind of dysfunctionality present in many Jewish families in which the parents or grandparents are Holocaust survivors. Many of these families are harsh, punitive, and judgmental. One might conclude that these people who survived the horrors of Nazism would be kinder, more understanding, and more loving. I'm sure some are, but many are not. This kind of family was my fishbowl. I never thought about it until one day I heard a therapist talking about collective trauma and recovery. We know what individual trauma does to people, but I never considered that an entire group could demonstrate the same characteristics. The more I looked, the more I saw, the more insight and understanding and compassion I developed. Managing my own dysfunctionality became easier and more effective. What is the trauma of slavery doing to today's African Americans? What will happen to the children of the Middle East when they raise their own children? What happened to the children of Cambodia? Do you have a culturally traumatic element in your own life? Does it affect your relationships in unexpected ways, including relationships with students?

Your Moments of Insight

- Make a list of moments you remember when you put it all together and realized why you needed to know something and how it affected you personally.
- Did these moments occur during your coursework? Your personal life?
- Do you ever make an effort to help your students make these connections? Should you? Would it change the quality of your teaching and their learning?
- Do you need a bit of skill training to feel comfortable engaging in this approach to learning?

6

PROFESSIONAL BOUNDARIES AND SKILLS

Searching for Meaning Is Not Counseling

If our civilization is built on a myth, to change our civilization we must change the myth. . . . We humans are meaning-making animals constantly seeking to make sense of the world. (Eisenstein, 2013, p. 213)

A major developmental task of all college students, regardless of age, is to make sense of the world and their place in it. In higher education a great deal of this effort occurs through contemplating the meaning and significance of subject matter in the disciplines and choosing a major or career path. Whenever faculty are asked to help students explore the personal meaning of subject matter, questions arise about connections between counseling and learning. Faculty are understandably reluctant to get into areas of personal vulnerability with students. Most are neither trained as nor interested in becoming counselors. Referring a student to the counseling center is a very good thing to do, but it may not address the cognitive elements of subjects that may have personal meaning for students. The student may be attempting to develop a sense of self-authorship, self-in-the-world, by incorporating information from the faculty member's discipline into his or her personal narrative. The notion that personal distress is a problem that must be passed on to a counselor rather than one that can be explored through introspection with a trusted mentor can be seen as an aspect of our academic fishbowl in which the personal is separated from the impersonal, meaning from information.

> The notion that personal distress is a problem that must be passed on to a counselor rather than one that can be explored through introspection with a trusted mentor can be seen as an aspect of our academic fishbowl in which the personal is separated from the impersonal, meaning from information.

Self-Authorship and the Creation of a Personal Narrative

Self-Authorship in Your Own Life

Do you remember the first time a person asked you to explain a perspective that you did not agree with? It might have been a compare-and-contrast assignment. It might have been explaining to your family something about a new friend from a "don't trust them" group. It might have been in a conversation about politics. The content isn't as important as the feelings you experienced. What if there were some merit to the other perspective? In my case, what if some People Who Drink are actually trustworthy and likeable? Would you want to discuss this with your family? I didn't.

Kegan (1994) calls composing one's own reality *self-authorship*. He describes self-authorship as "internally coordinating beliefs, values, and interpersonal loyalties rather than depending on external values, beliefs and external loyalties" (Baxter Magolda & King, 2004, p. xvii). A more expanded description of self-authorship really involves creating one's own narrative: Who does the student want to be in his or her world as it is imagined and projected into the future? Kegan's definition fits students best if they come from Euro-American backgrounds because *self* by implication means a single person. Students from collectivist cultures have different understandings of self that extend to families that are configured differently according to cultural background. The boundary between internal and external may also be located differently according to culture. Nevertheless, construction of one's narrative applies to all people—the creation of the story about who that person is and wants to be in cultural context. Students must decide whether the received narratives make sense in their current world. Usually when you ask students what they want their future to look like they can tell you, although the detail tends to fade as the timeline lengthens and the context broadens. Students want to be knowledgeable in their field of study and successful in their careers as defined both by financial success and by holding leadership positions. They usually want to create a family and to have a meaningful relationship with a partner, and to live in a place where they feel welcome and that offers good recreational and cultural opportunities. Students also want to fit into their larger communities and have a sense that their own lives matter in the greater scheme of things. Recently students have expressed a desire to have more positive cross-racial interactions with peers although only 39% stated that they had meaningful conversations about race outside class (Higher Education Research Brief, 2013). They are not interested in demonstrating for a cause but are slightly more interested in performing community service. Working on state and national campaigns interested only 8% of students in 2012 (Higher Education Research Brief, 2014). Much more information about student goals, values, and concerns can be found at the Higher Education Research Institute at UCLA, which has been collecting data on these issues for decades. The reason for exploring these values and student behaviors is to try to infer the current narratives that are shaping student lives and to investigate the connection between the narratives they have received and the ones they are inventing.

Primary personal narratives tend to come from family and immediate geographic/cultural community as well as faith community. All of these groups have stories that they tell their young people about the way the world works and how people of their particular group should expect to be treated by others (Ogbu, 1990). Some of these stories are productive and healthy; others, not so much. Family narratives include instructions about whether or not "people like us" go to college, own homes, and make friends with people from other groups; the role of family; and the expectations of family for loyalty among members. There are always stories about whom to trust among members of other groups and how to know whether a person is trustworthy. When students attend a college where the majority of faculty and administrative staff are members of a "You can't trust them" group, they have problems when they need help with class or other administrative issues. Frequently these groups, particularly students of color, have social/cultural clubs where older members provide mentoring to new students. Students who are first generation of European descent typically do not have this kind of support because they are invisible to each other. Personal narratives and expectations create multiple hurdles for students to overcome when attempting to succeed in college. This is a particularly difficult problem for first-generation students from all ethnic groups who also have no backup resources in their families or home communities, people who can help them understand what is expected or develop methods to solve problems. Faith communities are almost always helpful to students by providing emotional support, expressing confidence in the students, and reassuring them that their success will help the entire community. Unfortunately, many of these communities cannot provide mentoring because they have few members who attended college successfully.

Self-Authorship, Personal Narrative, and Counseling: What's the Difference?

"Who are you?" said the Caterpillar to Alice.
Alice replied rather shyly, "I hardly know Sir, just at present. At least I know who I was
when I got up this morning. But it must have changed several times since then."
(Carroll, 1898/1993, p. 27)

Self-authorship as related to learning has three aspects: cognitive maturity, an integrated identity, and mature relationships (Baxter Magolda & King, 2004, p. 6). *Cognitive maturity* is described as "intellectual power, reflective judgment, mature decision-making, and problem solving in the context of multiplicity" (p. 6). Reflective judgment and problem solving in the context of multiplicity both require that students can stand outside their narratives and understand that their system of understanding the world is just one system, not the Truth. If students retain the received authorship of their community narrative, they cannot do this. They will continue to search for the Right Answer, largely because realizing that there may be no Right Answer or that there may be reasons why several answers are partially right is so disconcerting. This realization is a self-authorship process. If your narrative of who you are changes, or even if it is subject to challenge, the results can be quite disorienting. Students often begin this process while attempting to complete "compare-and-contrast" assignments. Being forced to express two different points of view is very confusing if a person believes that only one opinion can be accurate. Role plays and debates also assist in the self-authorship process if students are expected to express perspectives that are not their own.

An *integrated identity* is "characterized by understanding one's own particular history, confidence, the capacity for autonomy and connection, and integrity" (Baxter Magolda & King, 2004, p. 6). Creating an integrated identity is an enormous challenge for most first-generation students and only slightly less so for other students. It's kind of a Humpty Dumpty experience. If their Narrative has told them that People Like Us don't go to college and these students attend college successfully, are they still the People Like Us? If the Don't Trust Them group runs the college, and the students actually find people there who help and support them, is that Selling Out? If they have an exam on the same day that they have family obligations and they miss the exam, would they have enough confidence to explain this problem to a professor, particularly a professor who has a different family/personal narrative?

Americans have psychologized our culture to an extreme degree. Everything that bothers a person seems to be a reason for Getting Help, a phrase that means seeking counseling, not getting a flat tire fixed or any other kind of help. We have also individualized most problems because we are a culture that privileges the framework of the decontextualized autonomous individual. Most cultures that emphasize the group (collectivist cultures) wouldn't think of Getting Help. Members think of talking to a relative, usually somebody who is older or more experienced in dealing with a particular problem. Problem solving is personal and relationship based. It doesn't require payment or insurance coverage. It's a thought process that has emotional elements to it, and it is not pathological. It's just an upsetting problem. After you discuss it with another person, you usually feel better and you Know What to Do. A person who can help students understand their personal history and the history of their group can usually do a fairly good job of helping students solve problems, including the problems generated by learning information that challenges the narratives they brought to college. This process of helping students place themselves in historical and cultural context is unusual in an academic setting, but it isn't difficult for anyone who teaches courses that students find disruptive to their own narratives. In this case, the professor knows the subject matter far better than the students and, in dialogue, can help them sort out the personal from the cultural issues. To do this, the professor needs to learn a few simple active listening skills and be able to overcome whatever personal discomfort may be experienced when engaging with students who are upset. These skills enhance productive conversation without leading to the personal anguish often brought to the surface in sessions with a counselor. See Appendix A for more about these skills.

A Morality Tale

When I was a freshman, drinking was prohibited in my residence hall. My friends had lots of ways to avoid discovery, but I was a threat to their activities because I always told The Truth. At the end of the year, there was a party in one room, and I wasn't invited because everybody was convinced that I would tell the RA what they had done. I discovered that the party had taken place because I saw the vodka bottles in the trash can outside the building the following morning. I was devastated. Here was my dilemma: I could stick to my Truth telling and have no friends or I could modify my idea of what was to be revealed and have friends. I rapidly developed a more nuanced idea about Truth telling. Truth telling was for Serious or Dangerous Issues where a person might get hurt. Nobody got hurt when a bunch of young women drank vodka in a dorm room. Voila! New criterion for my narrative. I could still be a Truth teller—I just had a more sophisticated understanding of ambiguity.

Before birth control or abortion had become legally available, I also had many serious conversations about sexual behavior that led to similar kinds of insights. These were very serious conversations because lots of my women friends were having sex with boyfriends. I learned that different people could have different ideas about moral behavior and that I didn't need to agree with all of them, or judge them. That was a huge learning experience. Was my perspective the only legitimate way to see things? If I asked my mother she would have said yes—but I didn't ask her.

Mature relationships constitute the final element of the connection between self-authorship and learning. As a person develops the ability to engage in mature relationships, the connections between self and others become more nuanced and require time for contemplation. As students develop mature relationships they also develop confidence in their own sense of identity. Chickering and Reisser (1993) describe this process as *increasing autonomy*, demonstrated by the ability to choose a course of action without the need for continuous reassurance from others. One way to see this process developing is to watch the ways students go to the cafeteria and eat their meals. First-year students rarely go to an eating place alone. They have to go with friends just to have the confidence to enter. As they get older, they learn to go to meals in smaller groups; sit with people they meet in the cafeteria; and, in rare instances, eat with people who aren't their immediate friends. Very few students sit alone.

Group Skills: A Focus on Process

Learning group skills is one context for learning how to balance self-authorship and collaboration. Students need to find their own Voice in any work group, but they also need to learn to collaborate. Often learning to collaborate involves learning to manage emotions, listen carefully, tolerate ambiguity, and analyze complex intellectual and interpersonal problems. Any course that involves conversations among students or group projects is an ideal venue for students to enhance their relationships with others who are different from themselves in meaningful ways. Students are often placed in groups where the work isn't evenly distributed or some people can't figure out how to cope with the work or interpersonal styles of other people. The consequences of this situation are typically that one high-achieving student does most of the work so that she or he can get a good grade—especially if everybody gets the same grade. Even though teaching students to work in groups is not part of most doctoral programs, it is an essential skill for most faculty. There are many ways to learn about groups. Most colleges have courses in group dynamics that might be open to interested faculty. People who teach those courses are often willing to do a short faculty development program for interested faculty so that they can learn and practice group skills. Helping students learn how to communicate and solve problems in groups is essential to many disciplines but can be learned only in a manner that integrates these interpersonal skills with the skills of the discipline. People cannot learn to manage their emotions (Chickering & Reisser, 1993) in a nonemotional environment. Emotions provide the content.

Mindfulness and Contemplation: A Focus on Meaning

When you are a Bear of Very Little Brain and you Think of Things, you find that sometimes a Thing which seemed very Thingish inside you is very different when it gets out into the open and has other people looking at it. (Sibley, 1986)

Contemplative skills are also crucial to developing mature relationships. These skills are less well known than group skills but are becoming more widely used in educational institutions at all levels (Barbezat & Bush, 2014). The purpose of contemplative skills is to stop the rational mind briefly so that students can access their emotions and the brain functions that make connections among disparate elements of information and areas of personal concern. These kinds of connections typically manifest in "aha" moments that professors find so reassuring as evidence of learning. Connections can be stimulated more frequently when the student is given the opportunity to "stop thinking," by substituting a noncognitive focus for a limited period. The most frequently used method for this kind of contemplation is called meditation. Meditation generally involves creating a strong but relaxed focus on a single phenomenon such as breathing, paying attention to the sounds in a room, or repetitive counting. This process derails the train of thought. It literally stops the internal narrative, whether that narrative is chanting "OMG, I don't understand!" or repeating the information for clarity or wondering what dinner will be tonight.

One type of meditation is called *mindfulness*, a practice that trains students to pay attention. This is an essential practice for wired students with distracted minds (Siegel, 2007). First, they must turn off all their devices. Then they do a mindfulness practice for a minute or two. Mindfulness practices can include repeating internal statements (e.g., "Calm yourself," "Imagine peace"), repeatedly counting backward from 20 to 0, doing a mental scan of one's body to identify areas of tension, or the ever-popular eating raisins or other small fruit while making an effort to focus completely on the sensations in the mouth. There are extensive lists of mindfulness practices on the Internet. Research indicates that the practice of mindfulness increases students' ability to focus their attention on both the cognitive elements of learning and the relationships they have with other students (Barbezat & Bush, 2014). Mindfulness practices are often introduced by the ringing of a meditation bell, a piercing but pleasant sound that also focuses attention. I do not recommend that anybody who isn't familiar with meditation try this in public, but if you are interested, get your own bell and practice with it until you are comfortable. Many meditation sites on the Internet sell these bells and have short clips of their different tones. My students love this approach. They all arrive in class late in the afternoon having worked all day. There is nothing they enjoy more than beginning a class with the opportunity to stop, shift focus away from the rest of their lives, and pay attention to what's happening in the classroom. It is a relaxing and opening process that supports learning. See Appendix B for more on contemplative practices in the classroom.

The consequence of all mindfulness practices is that they help students learn to observe their own internal narrative—the story they are telling themselves about the subject matter, the teacher, the other students, the meaning of whatever they are doing. This reflection process allows for the greater development of cognitive complexity and emotional control in relationship to both subject matter and working with other students. Mindfulness teaches students how to take a time-out before they speak or act; how to consciously relax when they feel tension rising; and how to frame their thoughts respectfully before they burst out with frustration, anger, or other destructive emotions (Goleman, 2003). Jon Kabat-Zinn (2012) has extensively documented the benefits of mindfulness practice. Students can focus on subject matter for longer periods of time, feel less stress about participating in class, express their opinions with less anxiety, and listen more carefully with less anxiety to differing opinions. As a professor, what more could you ask for? If you begin to use mindfulness practices in your classes, it is legitimate to suggest that students also practice at home, in a quiet spot. These practices require practice. The more a person engages in practice, the better it works and the easier it becomes to drop into that relaxed and focused state of mind.

All of these skills and practices have the possibility of stimulating student emotions, and many of these emotions are positive. Even when students get upset during meditation, awareness will probably diminish the distress and distraction that they experience as they are trying to learn. Use of these skills can be considered preparation for learning in the same way that we have learned that hungry children need to eat before they are ready to pay attention in class. If you want your students to focus on what you think they should learn, they have to stop focusing on all the other distractions present in their lives. This process becomes self-reinforcing as skill levels increase.

What's the Point?

What's the difference between helping students reflect on their life narrative and counseling them? I'm not sure I would want to split hairs about definitions on this subject. However, there are significant benefits to integrating the process of self-authorship into the learning process in any area of study:

- Learning is an integrated mind/body process. Ignoring any element of the cognitive/affective/meaning-making framework diminishes what students learn and their understanding of why it matters.
- Students who are self-authoring feel respected, listened to, and worthwhile. They don't feel "like a number" in class. When they

know that their opinions are considered worth exploring, they are more likely to be engaged in learning—even if they realize that they need better thinking skills to have more worthwhile opinions.

- When "not knowing" isn't considered the same thing as feeling worthless or stupid, students are more likely to admit what they don't know and think about what they're learning. They are also less likely to feel embarrassed about asking questions.
- Co-constructing knowledge does not mean giving students permission to engage in sloppy thinking or presenting unsupported opinions. It means creating an environment where opinions can be explored and students are not embarrassed by the fact that their opinion wasn't correct or that it didn't dominate the conversation. This is not about winning or losing arguments. It is about understanding different perspectives. Students learn to see each other as collaborators in the learning process, not competitors. They see personal and cultural perspectives as two of the many elements that can be considered when learning new information. For example, they can learn to discuss racial differences because they realize that people of different races have different experiences and that nobody's experience tells the whole story.

Ask yourself about your own experiences as a student and scholar. Have you been expected to internalize a narrative that says acknowledging emotions is inappropriate in academic settings? Does that approach work in your discipline? Are you concerned that if emotions are discussed you might not know what to do? You know how to do this, but you are not used to doing it in class. Talking with a friend about an emotional issue isn't counseling; it's listening and caring. Think about it. . . .

"Hallo, Rabbit. Is that you? . . . Let's pretend it isn't and see what happens." (Milne, 1926/1954, p. 104)

7

CURRICULUM, GENERAL
EDUCATION, AND THE
GRAND NARRATIVE

It seems best to consider that mind and matter are two dimensions of a single reality that
comes into being in an immense diversity of expression throughout the universe by some
self-organizing process. (Berry, 1999, pp. 25–26)

O nce again, we can circle back to our earlier questions. The questions for this chapter are: Why do students want to "get general
education requirements out of the way"?; and, of course, Why
do they consider so many of these requirements superfluous? What are
the possible connections between general education and support for
the self-authorship process? General education causes a great deal of
conflict in higher education and also consumes a great deal of faculty
time and energy (Bok, 2006). *General education* typically refers to a set
of required courses that the faculty of a particular university considers
essential to the education of its undergraduates. Embedded in the general education requirements is the faculty belief in whatever elements of
the Grand Narrative seem critical to producing "well-rounded" gradu-
ates. Of course, nobody has ever definitively described what a well-
rounded graduate knows, although many have tried (Bloom, 1987).
Rather than looking at our fishbowl, we are looking through it, from

many perspectives that are shaped by discipline, gender, age, faith tradition, and numerous other cultural elements. The first general education requirements were known as the Trivium (grammar, rhetoric, and logic) and the Quadrivium (arithmetic, music, geometry, and astronomy). These requirements constituted the entire curriculum of medieval universities and were considered the subjects that all educated men (*sic*) needed to know. These requirements were derived from the Greeks, particularly Socrates, Plato, and Aristotle, and their academies for the young men of Athens. Things have changed in the Western world, but not nearly as much as you might imagine.

We are still arguing about what it means to be an educated person, and what knowledge is essential for occupying whatever roles are reserved for educated people in the modern world. There are still many public roles that benefit from the perspective of an Educated Person and are often occupied by Uneducated People. For example, some of the recent challenges to science have come from public officials who have asserted that they do not believe in the accuracy of the evidence of climate change, that they believe that rape cannot lead to pregnancy, and that there is a correlation between skin color or sexual orientation and intelligence or human rights. People who cannot think clearly, assess the validity of knowledge, and make accurate connections between information and opinions about the meaning of the information are probably not the best people to serve in public office. Unfortunately, level of education or depth of understanding are not often criteria on which people base their votes in this democracy.

Of course, the world has changed since the Middle Ages and the Golden Age of Athens. Although there are many predictions, our world has become incredibly complicated and interactive. Nobody really knows with certainty how future unpredictable changes are likely to affect what people need to know or where they may learn it. There have been suggestions that universities have outlived their usefulness (Wood, 2014) or that we should adopt a system of "badges" based on acquisition of technical skills rather than a degree system that implies holders of degrees are well rounded. There it is again, the equivalency between roundedness and educated. What should a well-rounded student know?

General Education, Well-Rounded Students, and Poetic Insights

The answer to the previous question seems to depend on which rendition of the Grand Narrative operates in the consciousness of a particular collection of faculty members at a specific institution. The ancient Greeks decided what men (*sic*) needed to know based on their roles as citizens and their preoccupations with understanding the role of man in the universe. The medievalists were educating landowners, rulers, and priests, but the emphasis of the curriculum was less technical than persuasive, related to the roles of educated men as leaders. Who are we educating now and what roles will they occupy in our collective future and the future of our rapidly changing global, interconnected societies? The short answers are (a) everybody and (b) nobody knows. We are back in the middle of our conundrum, our ill-defined problem (King & Kitchener, 1994). It is time to look at the limits of our own fishbowl and understand how it shapes our view of the purpose of education, what knowledge is worth attaining, and how knowledge can be used to influence our world.

> *Inescapable romance, inescapable choice*
> *Of dreams, disillusion as the last illusion,*
> *Reality as a thing seen by the mind,*
> *Not that which is but that which is apprehended.*
> *(Stevens, 1964, "An Ordinary Evening in New Haven," p. 468)*

And, one might add, interpreted, because the purpose of organisms is to organize, and what humans organize is meaning (Parks, 2000). But why use poetry to enhance understanding?

> *The prologues are over. It is a question, now,*
> *Of final belief. So, say that the final belief*
> *Must be in a fiction. It is time to choose. (Stevens, 1964, "Oboe," p. 250)*

Beliefs create and color our fishbowls. Under our circumstances accuracy or consensual reality seems possible, but Truth remains an elusive metaphysical construct. Why use poetry to support the creation of insight? Poetry is one way of imposing or evoking order, of finding or shaping patterns, in the apparent chaos of daily life. Poetry is also helpful in supporting students as they decide what they think they need to know and what they think matters in life. There are other ways to find or impose order: mathematics, music, philosophy, art, cultural history, and so forth. Poetry is my way, but it is not the only way. When things moved more slowly than they do today, the older generation was presumed to provide reliable guidance for the younger generation. In this era we have no choice but to become self-authoring—all of us. As Bateson (1990) observed, "We have all become migrants in time" (p. 14); "We hold onto continuity, however profoundly it is flawed" (p. 8); "Fluidity and discontinuity are central to the reality in which we live . . . the ability to shift from one preoccupation to another and we are all vulnerable (because we can no longer be experts)" (p. 13).

Poetry is one of the arts of well roundedness. It brings the ability to broaden perspective and deepen insight. Science and technology achieve this capacity only at the most complex levels of understanding. Poetry, even in its most elementary form, can help provoke insight. "Twinkle, twinkle little star, how I wonder what you are" asks a significant question that can be addressed at many levels, from the technical to the philosophical. Poetry helps us see our fishbowl and perhaps create a new one, and, most surprisingly, we often don't know where the insight comes from. Poetry and literature, more broadly interpreted, is part of general education. Any subject that helps students address meaningful questions from a broad, "well-rounded" perspective is probably a candidate for inclusion in a general education curriculum. In this era, we have so much information and so many answers but we are not inclined to discus with our students methods of discerning important questions. In some cases, we are focusing on the answers we have instead of helping students master the skills of discovering new questions and learning to live with temporary answers. Daniel Barbezat, executive director of the Center for Contemplative Mind in Society (www.contemplativemind.org), compares students to speedboats. He says that today's students are high octane fast moving, and focused. They are moving at incredible speed but they have no rudder. They know how to move quickly but not how to choose direction (Barbezat, personal communication, October 12, 2012). The way we organize and present knowledge generally does not help students choose direction or create meaning because the way we teach, using disciplinary categories, generally does not reflect categories for creating meaning in human life. These categories reflect a consensus fishbowl idea of how to organize information. There is nothing wrong with organizing knowledge according to perceived patterns inherent in that knowledge. What is wrong is confusing the way we organize knowledge with the way students learn. This is another conundrum. We thought that those two issues were one but this is not typically the case.

> "Be patient toward all that is unsolved in your heart and try to love the questions themselves like locked rooms and like books that are written in a foreign tongue. Do not now seek the answers which cannot be given to you because you would not be able to live them. And the point is to live everything. Live the questions now. Perhaps you will then gradually, without noticing it, live along some distant day into the answer." (Rilke, 1934, pp. 34–35)

Looking at the Fishbowl, Not Through It

I am not sure how various faculties decide what should be included in general education requirements, but in many cases the choices may be more political than conceptual. Most general education programs use a scheme that is defined by several categories such as social sciences, humanities, physical and biological sciences, mathematics, writing, and other elements of literacy in both English and other languages. There are many variations. The current general education designation began when Charles William Eliot convinced the Harvard faculty to adopt the elective system in 1885. He cited two reasons for the transformation: (a) he believed that at some point boys (*sic*) needed to have the freedom to choose what they wanted to learn, and (b) knowledge was expanding exponentially to the point where college studies needed to be divided into general knowledge and discipline-based knowledge, an area that has become the "major." Prior to the adoption of the elective system, college graduation implied that most students knew most of the same information, organized somewhat like the Trivium and the Quadrivium (The Editors of the Encyclopaedia Brittanica, 2015). After Eliot transformed and fragmented the Harvard curriculum, faculties were left with the expanding challenge of deciding which elements of knowledge remained essential and which were optional. This challenge has become increasingly complex, leading us to the perennial question, What do students need to know? More accurately, from a faculty perspective, by the time they graduate, what do we expect them to know in all of the domains of study that we think are important in the modern world? The problem is that most of us view the issue of what students need to know from a variety of personal and cultural fishbowls. We do not often discuss our particular group of fishbowls or how they shape and reflect our value systems and analysis of cultural evolution as it pertains to higher education.

I am now repeating a list of ideas (from chapter 2) that Eisenstein (2013) describes as the "narrative of normal" as it operates in most of today's colleges and universities. The purpose of this repetition is to ask you to review the way undergraduate general education requirements are organized and taught in your institution. If this list seems like an accurate description of the ways your college conducts academic business, then you are looking at your own fishbowl.

- The allegiance to "objectivity" as a way of knowing.
- The assumption that subject perceives, but generally does not interact with, object.
- The separation of people from each other through concepts of individuality and autonomy.
- The fundamentally material nature of the universe.
- The separation of spirituality and materialism.
- The inappropriateness of discussing spiritual issues in most academic disciplines.
- The assumption that human beings have rights but that these rights do not generally extend to other living things or to the planet itself.
- The assumption that a major, if not sole, purpose of attending college is for students to learn career-related skills that will allow them to earn a good living (materially) by working in fields that are based on most of the aforementioned assumptions.
- The assumption that a major role of faculty is to ensure that students learn and can use these skills in work settings.
- The assumption that students are generally between the ages of 18 and 24 with limited life experience. They often make

decisions that harm themselves or others. It is generally not the role of faculty to get involved in this decision-making process or to help students examine the consequences of this behavior.

- The assumption that all things that students do outside the classroom are the responsibility of themselves or other adults employed in the university for purposes of helping students manage their lives (aka student affairs professionals).

Here are some of the operational implications of this list of ordinary assumptions:

- *Objectivity* implies that facts dominate most academic discussions and that facts are known and exist separately from the people who know the facts. This perspective excludes the co-construction of knowledge although it does not exclude the shaping of opinion based on facts. Objectivity can contribute to self-authorship but on its own does not help a student determine meaning or become engaged with new knowledge.
- *Subject/object interaction* implies that whatever subjective responses to the facts that may be present during a discussion of those facts ought to be excluded from consideration because subjectivity distorts objectivity. Emotional reactions to facts are very difficult to acknowledge in this context, much less integrate into a discussion. The worst part of this problem is that there are systems for including emotions in these kinds of conversations, but learning how to manage difficult conversations is typically not part of academic education for either faculty or students. We now know from brain science that suppressing emotions interferes with and does not support learning (Siegel, 2007). Once a student crosses the stress boundary, learning stops and self-defense takes over. That's a fact.
- *The fundamentally material nature of the universe and the exclusion of discussion of matters that have spiritual implications* reinforces the Cartesian fishbowl belief that has shaped much of our academic framework ever since. In a liberal democracy it is very difficult to discuss spiritual beliefs in secular settings, but it is perfectly possible to discuss self-authoring notions of value

and meaning. The Cartesian split between spirit and matter was challenged by Einstein when he said that "God doesn't play dice with the universe." Physicists and philosophers continue to explore the spirit/matter connection (Berry, 2009; Capra 1982, 1975; Palmer & Zajonc, 2010). This does not imply the right of any faith tradition or dogma to dominate. It simply implies that, when looking deeply, one may find order and derive meaning from a variety of perspectives.

- *The separation of people from each other* governs the way we assess learning. Collaboration without permission is called cheating in this culture. In our world of collaborative work and decision making, does this approach still make sense as the only way to assess learning? Is there a better way? Should we be teaching the skills of group analysis and conflict resolution along with "the facts"? How much money do you think we spend on bubble sheets every year?

- *The purpose of attending college is career preparation.* Every faculty member in the general education fields has suffered from the consequences of this belief, which degrades the value of self-authorship, the co-construction of knowledge, and the role of values and emotions in learning. Most of us would rather discuss the cost of building a new parking garage or the status of campus athletics than the role of emotions and values in learning. This is true even though we know that students don't learn what they don't care about and that emotions are critical to the learning process. Those are facts (Siegel, 2007).

- *Learning that occurs outside the classroom (i.e., finding patterns of meaning, developing healthy relationships, choosing meaningful careers) is not in my job description. Other people, aka student affairs professionals, do that.* This belief prevents all of us from sharing what we know about learning and impedes the effectiveness of the learning processes that occur in many locations. When was the last time you discussed learning with a member of the student affairs staff? Do you know anybody on the student affairs staff? What happens in your own discipline when new knowledge is developed? You learn it—or at least learn something about it. Now we have new knowledge about learning. Maybe it's time to pick up some of this knowledge and these skills as well. Information about the basic skills and links to additional learning appear in Appendix B.

> When was the last time you discussed learning with a member of the student affairs staff? Do you know anybody on the student affairs staff?

Organizing the General Education Curriculum for Self-Authorizing Learning

It is time to reconsider what each of us thinks students need to know and to ask students what they think they need to know. The Higher Education Research Institute at UCLA (www.heri.ucla.edu) is probably one of the best sources to answer that question in general. The Indiana University Center for Postsecondary Research (www.cpr.iub .edu) is also a good source of general information. When it comes to developing general education requirements, general knowledge about student concerns, along with the general knowledge that curriculum committees have about developing needs in our evolving world, is essential. These areas of knowledge include economic interdependence, climate change, the need for people from different cultures to learn to work together and understand each other, technological development, migration and refugee patterns, and epidemiology, to name a few. They are all interdisciplinary and all involve some elements of learned reflection and collaboration in order to be considered valuable by students. The list is endless, but it should be clear that most faculties have experts in the key areas that should be considered in curricular reform. The most important element of this discussion is the realization of the need to have this conversation before requirements are identified and organized. It is too late to rearrange the deck chairs on the *Titanic*. The old categories for general education reflect methods of organizing knowledge. They do not reflect the ways we use knowledge to address issues of critical concern to all of us, particularly students. Does it make sense to use the elective/ cafeteria approach that reinforces fragmentation and does not give students the opportunity to reflect and integrate? The key questions resurface: What is important for our students to know understand, and use as they face their collective future? Why do we think these things are important? Do we have the skills to listen to drastically different viewpoints and manage our emotions so that we can come to consensus? Or to live with the reality that there may be no consensus? In short, can we use the group skills we must expect and teach our students to use? Can we self-author new knowledge frameworks that reflect our evolving era?

Different Ways of Organizing Curricula

Thomas Berry (1999), in his book *The Great Work,* addressed curriculum organization from a very different perspective. He evaluated the consequences of our old narrative and looked at the planetary and interpersonal exploitation that it has engendered. He suggested that what colleges should teach is a new story of the universe that would be integrated and life enhancing. Eisenstein (2013), in *The More Beautiful World Our Hearts Know Is Possible,* conducted the same kind of analysis at much greater length with much greater attention to the contributions of each of our historical disciplines. Both authors concluded that the systems that support life on our planet are collapsing, much more quickly than we realize, and that higher education can contribute to turning this process around—but only if we change the way we teach, the way we organize what we expect students to learn, and if we give credence to the cocreation of knowledge. The problem is the Rabbit Hole. Once we begin thinking the way these two authors suggest and the way I have suggested throughout this book, we have fallen down a rabbit hole and nothing will ever look the same. Nobody likes to be disoriented. Self-authorship requires and implies disorientation. The sources of authority in the collective universe shift like an earthquake. This kind of shift requires a great deal of emotional discipline to maintain any kind of stability. As Wordsworth warned us, intellectual understanding alone is not enough:

> *Books! 'tis a dull and endless strife:*
> *Come, hear the woodland linnet,*
> *How sweet his music! on my life,*
> *There's more of wisdom in it. . . .*

Our meddling intellect
Mis-shapes the beauteous forms of things:—
We murder to dissect.
Enough of Science and of Art;
Close up those barren leaves. . . . (Wordsworth, 1798/1962, pp. 74–75)

Barbara McClintock, a highly regarded geneticist, expressed a similar notion when she talked about the way she thought about her studies of the genetics of corn. She talked about a process she compared to leaning into, or listening to, the organism to infer an understanding of its genetic functioning (Keller, 1983). Her method of developing insight was mocked by other geneticists, but her work was groundbreaking. Both Arnold and McClintock were suggesting holistic and intuitive approaches, he as the sole way of understanding and she as a complementary method.

Once again, things have changed since Wordsworth. His expression in these phrases assumes a dualistic way of thinking. We no longer need to murder to dissect. We can take three-dimensional pictures. We can use both/and thinking. The same is true of the approach developed by McClintock. She was an expert in data description and analysis, but she was also aware of the larger patterns that shaped her research and the genetic patterns of corn. We can learn facts and still take time to consider their consequences. We can read poetry and learn calculus. But if we step into that process of connecting thinking, feeling, and reflecting, we will fall down the Rabbit Hole with no guarantee that things can ever feel correct again.

Do you remember the first time your belief in authority shifted?

- What happened, where were you, who else was involved?
- How did your ideas change?
- How did your feelings change?
- How did your relationships change?
- How long did it take before you settled into the new perspective?

****

- I am asking you to challenge the authority of the ways you were taught, your beliefs about knowledge, the value of your

> professional expertise, and the appropriate boundaries of what
> you permit yourself to discuss with students.
> - This is a huge Rabbit Hole.
> - You will probably need some additional training.
> - Can you handle it?

In the Rabbit Hole Almost Anything Can Make Sense

"Get to your places," shouted the Queen in a voice of thunder and people began running about in all directions, tumbling up against each other: however they got settled down in a minute or two and the game began. (Carroll, 1865/1993, p. 55)

Alice had a lot of trouble in this unusual game of croquet. The balls were live hedgehogs, and the mallets were live flamingos. She had a lot of trouble managing her flamingo. We all have a lot of trouble managing any living, changing thing. If we have a narrative that privileges control, objectivity, and linearity, we tend to get embarrassed about our lack of control (Palmer & Zajonc, 2010). However, if we have a narrative that privileges the exploration of multiple perspectives and maintenance of core values in the midst of shifting circumstances, we are simply practicing our craft and helping students to co-construct meaning.

Berry (1999) suggests that the curriculum should be organized so that students can learn and envision "the story of the universe" (p. 81). He asserts that "the entire world is composed of subjects to be communed with, not primarily objects to be exploited" (p. 82). Zajonc, a noted physicist and philosopher, expresses the same perspective: "No relationship-free, true state of affairs exists. . . . We need to learn to see (objects) as existing through relationships with the observer," not as things in themselves (Palmer & Zajonc, 2010, p. 67). This perspective on relationships among objects and events is a radical shift from an emphasis on objects as singular. Eisenstein (2013) expresses his notions of our grand narrative as a new Story of the World, "a matrix of narratives, agreements and symbolic systems that comprises the answers our culture offers to life's most basic questions" (p. 4). None of these authors suggests that one perspective should dominate what we think about ourselves, our communities, our environments, and our place in the cosmos. They privilege relationship, connectedness, contemplation, and evolution. There are no bubble sheets in this world. Everybody needs to know how to sail, read a compass, and work together. The more experienced sailors support and guide those with less experience.

> We cannot control the wind but we can learn to shift our sails.

Berry's story would be organized to explore three aspects of our collective world, "observational science, a developmental universe [and] an inner self-organizing capacity" (1999, p. 24). Certainly this approach could make as much sense as "general education, major, electives" or "five courses in the social sciences, three in the physical sciences and mathematics, and four in the humanities." People and the culture that supports categories are their creators. Anything that has been created can be re-created. Our problem is that our academic categories have been in place for so long that they look like geologic formations. Studies in the disciplines support the major categories of exploration because they provide a great deal of the content and most of the research paradigms or ways of knowing. The problem with the traditional ways of creating categories of requirements is that students don't know where they come from or why they matter, so the entire order of studies seems like nothing more than a check-off list. It would be much easier for students to understand Berry's three groupings and then for faculty to explain how the different areas of study might fit into each group, preserving choice but limiting meaninglessness.

What if . . .

- The first required courses that all students took were organized around the question, "What do you think you need to know and who do you think you want to be?"
- First-year experience courses asked students to address that question, explore the campus for possible resources, and then share their answers with each other?
- Students were asked to write the story of how the world works that they received from their families and to share those stories

in respectful ways so that each would understand that others
did not have the same upbringing or expectations?
- Students were asked to imagine the lives they wanted for
themselves and their families and then investigate the ways
they could go about creating those lives, using their college as
a major resource?
- Self-authorship and contributing to the lives of others were
seen as two sides of the same process?

Then . . .

- How would your teaching change if any of this happened?
- What kind of additional training would you like to have? (See
the appendices to learn more about facilitation and contemplation methods in the classroom.)

Create Your Own Rabbit Hole

Einstein famously said that our problems "cannot be solved at the same
level of thinking that created them" (as cited in Eisenstein, 2013, p.
96). We need to create some new rabbit holes, or find out what other
rabbit holes, or systems of meaning making, or stories about the way
the world works currently exist in our world but are not dominant in
the Grand Narrative of the West. Eisenstein refers to the ancient Story
of Separation that precedes the Grand Narrative and comprises most of
its foundation. He suggests creating a Story of Reunion and offers an
approach that helps students learn some of the ancient wisdom from
indigenous tribes and the sacred stories of many traditions as a way to
help modern students create a story of reunion for their own world.
In current language, that would come from the anthropology and literature requirements but would be framed as a way to organize one's
thinking about life after graduation. For example, how would we think
about the value of using a vision quest experience as part of a student's
capstone process? Could a vision quest be considered a cultural variation of a capstone project? On the level of symbolic significance, could
we adequately describe the difference between spending four days in
front of a computer "thinking" and four days on a mountaintop doing

something like thinking, but culturally different from writing a paper? It seems as if both exercises have a similar purpose, but they are not considered equally valid in the current educational context (Grande, 2004).

I teach a course called "Program Design in Student Affairs," referred to colloquially as "Create Your Own College." Students are given a college type (private liberal arts, historically Black, faith based, tribal, community or technical, public university) and asked to create an integrated undergraduate curriculum. This curriculum integrates disciplines and experiential learning. In the skills component, students must learn group skills, leadership, communicating across lines of significant difference, and creating sustainable environments. Students have created some fascinating ways to organize undergraduate education:

- Eastern Detroit University served the population of Detroit. It had a child care center where early childhood students could care for the children of the adult population who were also students. Students created an auto design and repair center that provided low-cost auto maintenance and engineering education. They used information from all areas of study to design a transportation system to bring students who didn't own cars to the campus. Buildings on campus were green, food from the cafeteria was recycled or distributed to homeless shelters, and wastewater was recycled in a variety of ways. Every project had academic aspects, and the practical application of subject matter was integrated into appropriate courses and internships.
- Grandin College, named after noted educator Temple Grandin, was designed to maximize the success of autistic students in many disciplines while serving as a training ground for other students who want to support people on the autism spectrum in schools, work environments, and community life.
- Kenahten University, a tribal college, was organized as a circle with the major components of the student experience being "Community Engagement, Academic Performance, Service Learning, and Nurturing of the Spirit." The entire structure of the college was framed according to tribal beliefs and values, with the academic disciplines embedded within the larger

meaning structure. Time for silent reflection and the creation of group story was also part of the learning experience, as befits the culture of the tribal members who attended this college.

- The purpose of Isaac Myers College, named after an industrialist of African descent in Baltimore, was to create an "intellectually curious residential community of scholars centered on a better understanding of global complexities. Our distinct liberal arts education works to inspire leaders through transformative learning opportunities promoting critical thinking, diversity, and self-awareness" (Isaac Myers Mission Statement, 2013 class project). Requirements were organized around academic progress, community engagement, personal experience, and reflection that integrated the student experience through seminars, journaling, and personal life planning for self-authorship. All students had to learn the skills of personal decision making, financial management, support of their work and the institution, and conflict management, as well as find ways to contribute to the larger community. Each also had to complete a capstone project that mapped out the beginning stages of their after-college lives.

These projects have been created over the past 15 years, as I have learned to teach the course in ways that stimulate student creativity. Few of the students expect to see these colleges become operational, but they all know that they can imagine different ways to organize learning, and that is the point.

Now What?

We began this conversation with several major points:

- The Grand Narrative shapes most of our undergraduate curricula and institutions. We don't even know the effects it has on all of our business because it has become an invisible fishbowl.
- A very important element of this narrative is the subject/object split and the belief that emotions interfere with learning by distorting objectivity and accuracy.

- Nobody learns anything if it doesn't matter to the person. We learn to repeat information but we do not retain it or understand why it is important.

We also know that student success is a very important issue at this time; that attrition in most four-year institutions is above 50% after two years; that students are distracted, preoccupied with many aspects of their lives that have nothing to do with school; and that their finances are one of the major sources of stress in their lives. Faculty are frustrated. Students are frustrated. One key to addressing these problems is down the rabbit hole. The exploration might be confusing but the results are very likely to be fruitful. The missing element is courage—and that can be supplied only by the people who are willing to take the journey.

8

ASSESSMENT

Documenting Learning From Alternate Perspectives

Peter Troiano

Assessment of student learning has been a cornerstone of the American educational system. Learners have been expected to demonstrate mastery of basic content in order to move to a more advanced level of discipline-specific learning. The system is predicated on a sequential structure, as evidenced by course levels and prerequisites, with success measured in terms of the learner's progress toward completion. Further, learning is viewed as a cumulative process facilitated by the development of higher ordered thinking skills. The more adaptable a learner can become and the more advanced a learner's capacity to deal with the complexities of the world around the learner, the higher the potential for advanced levels of thinking and learning.

The Assessment Process

Traditional measures of student learning, including quizzes, tests, comprehensive exams, and oral defenses, place the responsibility for learning squarely on the shoulders of the learner. Historically, demonstration of content mastery has been viewed as the learner's responsibility with very little expectation placed on the teacher other than to deliver the content in whatever way deemed most appropriate. However, a movement spurred by the increasing costs, constricting budgets, declining enrollments, and competing for scarce resources has ushered in an era of increased accountability. As a result, educators are facing increased pressure to design comprehensive student learning outcomes to measure content mastery, as well as higher order thinking skills, and to demonstrate positive progress toward achievement of stated outcomes.

Instructors responsible for transmitting knowledge and facilitating learning through traditional and nontraditional classroom settings are not the only professionals under close scrutiny. In keeping with the increased emphasis on experiential and integrated learning, student affairs professionals also have a responsibility to facilitate student learning and to develop student learning outcomes goals. There is widespread agreement in present-day college and university settings that learning is not just a classroom activity. Students learn about the world as well as themselves through their involvement in out-of-classroom activities, and learning occurs in student unions, residence halls, and wellness centers as much it does in libraries, laboratories, and classrooms (Keeling, 2008). Given this widely held view, all learning, in and out of the classroom, must be designed and assessed using an outcomes-based model in order to support the assertion that learning is, in fact, taking place.

The majority of colleges and universities in America, more than three fourths, report that they have a common set of intended learning outcomes for all undergraduate students (Hart Research Associates, 2009). The skill areas mentioned most often are writing, critical thinking, quantitative reasoning, and oral communication, consistent with those employers say they would like to see colleges and universities address. Despite institutions placing a strong emphasis on communicating these learning outcomes to students, most administrators concede students on their campuses have a limited awareness and understanding of them (Arum & Roksa, 2011).

Institutions differ in terms of their stated learning outcomes depending on the mission of the institution, the complexity of the organizational structure, and the changing demographics of their student population. Some institutions conduct assessments on all undergraduate students, regardless of major or career choice, according to a uniform set of standards, whereas others have set an expectation that each academic department will design its own set of learning outcomes and assessments based on discipline-specific criteria. In many cases, institutions have developed one set of outcomes that applies specifically to general education requirements and another set that applies to the overall undergraduate experience (Hart Research Associates, 2009). The tools and methods used to assess student learning outcomes vary by institution as well. Traditional methods are being replaced by more emergent tools and methods such as rubrics, student surveys, e-portfolios, capstone courses, and a range of integrated processes known as authentic assessments. Authentic assessments include systematic analysis of student journals and observation of student behavior either in field laboratory settings or in assessment centers. Alverno College pioneered authentic assessment by creating assessment centers that students could visit when they thought they had mastered a particular skill required for graduation. Elon College has created a range of assessment scales that allow students to report increases in their sense of meaning and purpose in their lives, descriptions of how they spend their time, and pre-post assessments of the value of specific courses in helping them articulate their own life goals (Felten, personal communication, October 10, 2014; Felten 2014a, 2014b).

Operationalizing Assessment in All Its Complexities

A few years ago, a group of faculty and staff at a large and rather complex university decided to embark on a comprehensive assessment project. The campus had undergone a significant change in senior leadership, and new leaders recognized that assessment had not been made a priority for some time. Two members of the university's newly formed assessment team attended a workshop in Washington, DC, designed to assist higher education professionals in developing assessment plans for their campuses. The program was sponsored by the Council for the Advancement of Standards in Higher Education (CAS), an organization comprising 39 member organizations and a constituency of more than 100,000 professionals, whose mission is to provide higher education professionals with tools to assess institutional effectiveness and student learning outcomes (CAS, 2006).

As part of its mission, CAS has put forward six broad categories of student learning and development that all higher education professionals should be committed to fostering in students: knowledge acquisition, construction, integration, and application; cognitive complexity; intrapersonal development; interpersonal competence; humanitarianism and civic engagement; and practical competence. It is expected that individual and organizational members will create a plan to identify, operationalize, and assess desired student learning outcomes and to articulate how their programs and services contribute to student learning and development.

CAS is not the only organization that has put forward a set of student learning objectives intended to serve as a guide for assessment and practice. *Learning Reconsidered: A Campus-Wide Focus on the Student Experience* (National Association of Student Personnel Administrators & American College Personnel Association [NASPA & ACPA], 2004) suggests seven broad categories of student learning outcomes. These seven categories are similar to those endorsed by CAS: cognitive complexity; knowledge acquisition, integration, and application; humanitarianism; civic engagement; interpersonal and intrapersonal competence; practical competence; and persistence and academic achievement. Several dimensions further illuminate each category, and developmental experiences, sometimes referred to as developmental tasks, add meaning and provide direction (NASPA & ACPA, 2004).

The Association of American Colleges and Universities (AAC&U) has also adopted a set of key outcomes around which all students, regardless of major or academic background, should demonstrate proficiency during their undergraduate studies (AAC&U, 2005). These outcomes include a range of subject matter and skills such as knowledge of human culture and the natural world, intellectual and practical skills, and individual and social responsibility. Knowledge of human culture and the natural world includes discipline-specific knowledge in the student's chosen field of study and in the liberal arts. Intellectual and practical skills includes written and oral communication, critical and creative thinking, quantitative and information literacy, teamwork, and integration of learning. Individual and social responsibility includes civic engagement, ethical reasoning, intercultural knowledge, and propensity for lifelong learning. AAC&U recommends that institutions committed to setting standards for measuring student learning outcomes set clear goals, establish programs and lines of responsibility for achieving those goals, teach creatively and effectively, and assess to ensure that all students are learning. This can be accomplished through the following critical steps: (a) orienting students to expectations, (b) developing a plan of study for each student, (c) conducting milestone assessments, and (d) implementing a capstone or culminating experience. Learning outcomes formulated by these associations are not discipline specific. They are related to overall sense of campus mission.

At the conclusion of the workshop, the two new assessment staff members returned to their campus armed with the knowledge and tools to launch the assessment project as planned. To generate enthusiasm for the project and to achieve a level of commitment across the institution that would be necessary to carry the project forward, one of the keynote speakers from that conference in Washington, DC, was invited to campus for a one-day workshop. This facilitator spent the morning speaking to invited faculty and student affairs staff members about the importance of assessment. The second half of the day was spent with department heads assisting them in developing and refining student learning outcomes.

As the day wore on, participants in the workshop began to show signs of anxiety and frustration. While facilitators attempted to keep the group focused on writing student learning outcomes and on developing ways to measure progress toward mastery of these outcomes, progress was impeded by a sense of dread that threatened to derail the entire process. Not surprisingly, there was a certain amount of resistance to the work of building a comprehensive assessment plan. Although some attendees recognized the need to engage in this effort and demonstrated a moderate degree of excitement for the project, many expressed concern for the way the work would be carried out on their campus. In a debriefing meeting immediately following the session, facilitators assured the leadership team that what they were hearing from the group was not that different from what they often heard when they visited with faculty and staff on college campuses to discuss assessment.

Staff members were concerned about the amount of extra work and time this project would require. Many commented that their plates were already too full and that adding this additional responsibility would mean they would have to spend less time actually engaged in the practice of facilitating student development and learning. One team member went so far as to ask what he should tell his staff when they raised this concern, as he was certain they would. The response the expert presenter provided rang true for the leadership team and still resonates today, although it did not sit well with many of the participants that day. In a matter-of-fact and nonjudgmental way, the facilitator responded, "Tell them to get a bigger plate." By rewriting job descriptions, restructuring responsibilities, and rethinking performance appraisal criteria, assessment can be made a basic expectation and a primary responsibility of all educators. Maki (2004) acknowledges the extensive adaptation process that many educators must experience as they learn that we now live in a culture of assessment and accountability and cannot simply refuse to participate if they wish to remain engaged in higher education. Legislators and other oversight boards have also become accountable to their own set of stakeholders and need data both to convince and to be convinced that the money being spent on learning is actually producing learning. The process of committing to a systematic culture of assessment must be institution-wide and integrated into the reward structure.

Prior to this transformation there was a fairly common understanding that student development and learning was happening and that no proof should be necessary. Department heads were often offended that their professional judgment was being challenged. Staff members who had been receiving favorable evaluations from supervisors and positive feedback from students regarding their work developed a defensive posture as they expressed concern over the need for more formal assessments. It is important for higher education professionals to understand that although they are recognized for their ability to facilitate student learning and development in informal ways through their day-to-day contact with students, a more formal process for identifying and quantifying student learning outcomes is absolutely essential. Komives and Smedick (2012) point out, "Utilizing standards to guide program design along with related learning outcomes widely endorsed by professional associations and consortiums can help provide credibility and validity to campus specific programs" (p. 78).

Finally, participants expressed discomfort over the data that might be uncovered through this process and fear over how data might be used to evaluate job performance. Even members of the group who exhibited the highest levels of confidence in their ability to educate students seemed to be distrustful of the process. Herein Les one of the "dualisms" regarding assessment (Love & Estanek, 2004) that can often impede the process: assessment for improvement and assessment for accountability. If assessment is viewed as a way to justify distribution of resources or to prove that one is an effective practitioner and not as a way to provide continuous improvement of programs and services, we are confusing assessment and evaluation.

When conducted properly, assessment lends credibility to the work at hand and demonstrates to others that higher education professionals are doing what it is they say they do: facilitate student learning and development in the college populations they serve. In this era of almost universal demand for accountability, the presence of many underprepared students, and limits on budgets in all of our institutions, beginning the dialogue about assessing learning outcome and setting learning goals has become essential. There is no deadline for any institution to initiate or implement this process. However, it is becoming increasingly clear that institutions that can present credible data to funding sources are doing better than institutions that are not able to do so.

The Inevitability of Assessment in the Current Environment

Assessment is an approach to gathering and analyzing data. It is a learning process. As in all the other kinds of learning processes described throughout this book, disorientation is inevitable. We are asking both faculty members and student affairs professionals to document student learning in a manner that supports our assertions about education and its value to students and the larger society. The principles of engaged learning described throughout this book also apply to this type of learning. If the goal is to create a culture of assessment, documentation, and accountability on our campuses, the process must somehow connect to the self-images of the people who are expected to participate. Just telling them to do it isn't enough, just as telling students to remember and calling that process "learning" isn't enough. The narrative of higher education is shifting in what amounts to a cultural sea change. There are some waves in the fishbowl. The value and purpose of higher education in an increasingly technological society is being questioned as never before. We are collecting Big Data in incomprehensible quantities. Collecting the data is a technological skill. Understanding the data, knowing what questions to ask, and figuring out what the data mean and how they should be used involves critical thinking skills and that takes us right back to general education. The important thing to realize is that the problem isn't "either/or." The world is complex, and dualistic methods of posing problems have limited value. Students need to be able to learn information and know why the information matters in the many worlds they inhabit. All of us need to be able to switch from poetry to statistics. Faculty need to articulate learning goals, assess learning outcomes, and place their particular segment of the learning process into the larger framework of their own institution. As faculty we are now expected to expand our own learning processes from learning information in our discipline to learning how to help students with the process and finally to demonstrate that we have done what we said we intended to do. It's not a mystery but it is a lot of hard work.

> "It just shows what can be done by taking a little trouble," said Eeyore. "Do you see, Pooh? Do you see, Piglet? Brains first, then hard work." (Sibley, 1986, p. 7)

CONCLUSION . . . WELL,
MAYBE NOT

A book that begins by documenting the erratic academic career of its author and asserts that her inquiry method involves going around in circles doesn't exactly require a conclusion. In fact, a conclusion may not be appropriate because this narrative implies an ongoing conversation. However, I have written this book in an effort to elucidate some of the underlying issues that make it very difficult to change the ways we teach college students and organize our universities. I have always been more interested in the why than in the how of things. My personal belief is that if you understand why circumstances are the way they are, you are in a better position to reframe understanding of the causes and therefore change the experience.

Many years ago Joel Barker (1992) described "the paradigm effect" in which he discussed the mental filtering that occurs when evidence in the environment does not fit the explanatory paradigm of the person who perceives it. Barker's notion was that a problem that seemed insoluble when viewed through one paradigm actually disappeared when viewed through an alternative frame of reference. This is another way of saying that if you change your assumptions, your outcomes will be different. The good news is that becoming aware of paradigms, or fishbowls, helps us challenge or question our fundamental assumptions about difficult problems. The bad news is that when we engage in this process we lose much of our previous skill set and expertise. *The Saber-Tooth Curriculum* (Peddiwell, 1939) described this process in great detail. When saber-tooth lions roamed a particular part of the world, the educators in that world developed a curriculum to help students survive life that was menaced by saber-tooth creatures, who considered human beings potential food sources. When the saber-tooth lions became extinct, the curriculum developers didn't notice. As the years went on, life in school using the saber-tooth curriculum became more and more difficult because the skills were no longer necessary, the background information had become irrelevant, and the outdated curriculum did not help students understand or live well in their current environment. I'm sure you get my point.

Much of the approach to curriculum and institutional organization currently in use is as outdated as the saber-tooth curriculum. The real problem is that we are in an unprecedented situation. Our structures of teaching and methods of organizing student learning are grounded in the mid-nineteenth century. One might even say they are grounded in the twelfth century if Oxford University is our touchstone. We need to move toward new methods of understanding learning; new approaches to engaging students in the learning process; and, of course, new methods of organizing our institutions to accomplish these goals. We need a different paradigm that includes self-authorship and personal conversations about meaning in the teaching/learning process as these new methods unfold. There is a great deal of scientific evidence that this approach is effective and compatible with what we already know about learning in college. However, the paradigm in which we are all immersed makes believing this new evidence very difficult. Everybody seems to be too busy to give this subject serious thought at the level of the narrative. As a result our collective belief systems make change difficult and impede our ability to bring our institutions in line with societal needs and expectations. We also have significant societal problems around racial and economic injustice, ecological catastrophes and climate change, and a widespread sense of personal helplessness in addressing these very important issues. Higher education is one site in our culture where these problems can be engaged in a meaningful way for an entire generation of students. For better or worse, these issues will be engaged by current students only if we find ways to help them learn that are more engaging and that allow them to see that what they are doing has much broader implications than simply getting a better job. The job they hope to get may not be there. The world they hope to live in will not be what it is right now. The most powerful tool that we have as educators to turn this *Titanic* around is to reconsider the ways we teach and align our methods with the ways students learn and live. If we can do that, I will not despair and neither should you. Now is the time to start talking to each other about the fishbowl paradigm and its limits. We are all journeying together toward an unknown and largely unpredictable future.

There is an African proverb that seems appropriate to end/begin this conversation: *If you want to go fast, go alone. If you want to go far, go together.* Teaching our students in ways that help them learn to talk about problems, use what they know, and solve problems for the greater good seems like a wise approach. I would add a sentence to the proverb: *If you don't know where you're going, it's good to be with friends and go together.*

APPENDIX A

WORKING IN GROUPS AND FACILITATING DISCUSSIONS

Some students are good at helping groups work together, address conflicts, and solve problems. Some aren't. Teaching students group skills is not typically part of any academic discipline, but the work environment requires that students learn to use these skills effectively.

Group Composition

- Do not let students pick their own groups.
- Be aware of seating patterns before you set up the groups so you can split up friendship groups if appropriate.
- Before groups begin work, ask them to introduce themselves and share contact information.

Group Process Issues

- Ask students in their groups to discuss the best and the worst group they ever belonged to. Then have them report their findings to the class and draw some general conclusions about what makes a group work well. Summarize this list of effective behaviors and write the list on a whiteboard or blackboard and/or post it online. It is also illuminating to have a classroom discussion about why these behaviors make a group work. You definitely do not need to be the expert. You just need to listen, summarize, and if appropriate ask the students how this approach to group work might help them in their careers. This discussion might even provide an opportunity for a grad to come to class and talk about work environment or for the students to talk about places where they have worked.

- Ask students within their groups to discuss how they handle conflicts or what they do when they really disagree with somebody, report their findings, and discuss good conflict management strategies. If you need support in the conflict management strategies area, try searching the topic online, inviting a member of the student affairs staff to co-teach that class, or find a partner on the faculty who is experienced in this area.

- Have each group pick an easy to use signal for stopping work when somebody feels ignored. This can be as simple as saying, "I'm stuck."

Group Facilitation Skills (for the Professor)

There are at least two keys to effective group facilitation. One is *active listening* and the other is *observing group dynamics*.

Active Listening

- When you listen to what students are saying, try not to think about what you are going to say afterward. Listen with a clear mind (see Appendix B) and listen for themes. Then tell the students what you have heard or seen. For example, "You seem to be confused about who's at fault in the Palestinian-Israeli conflict. You seem to want to place the blame on one of the groups." Rephrasing what the student said before responding assures the student that you have understood the student's intended meaning. The student is then more open to listening to new information. This process creates the beginnings of a dialogue.

- Encourage students to speak with each other rather than to you alone. For example: "Jorge, that was an interesting idea. Susan, you seemed to react to what Jorge said. What do you think about the idea? Anybody else want to respond?" I think of this aspect of group facilitation as weaving. You want to teach the students to listen to each other because it builds trust, encourages self-authorship, and teaches them how to treat differences of opinion respectfully. After you have exhausted a particular topic, summarize what you think you heard. For example: "It sounds as if you are concerned about being misunderstood or not being able to express yourself accurately. Some of you may be concerned about being attacked or dismissed for your opinions." Then ask the students if you got it right or missed anything important.

Observing Group Dynamics

- Watching group dynamics is like watching a pot of soup heat up. As the soup gets hotter you can see currents and bubbles in the pot. These currents affect the various ingredients in the soup differently depending on their density, size, and so forth. You can also see dynamics in any body of water by watching currents and the objects floating in the water. If you like to fish you have seen this phenomenon. If you haven't noticed, perhaps you should go fishing. Once you experience dynamics in fluid, try watching a department meeting. Similar phenomena occur.
- In your classes begin observing the connections among your students—either positive or negative. When some students speak, everybody listens. Others seem to evoke eye rolling, looking down or toward each other, or arm crossing. If there are out-of-class alliances in the group students may speak in an invariant order. For example, as soon as Kemesha speaks, her friend Jamal may follow up. If people ignore Kemesha, Jamal may get agitated. If students have competitive relationships or are trying to outspeak each other, the follow-up is likely to be a contradiction or a challenge. There are gender patterns to this

phenomenon as well (Belenky, Clinchy, Goldberger, & Tarule, 1986).

- Be aware that sometimes the professor is the target of the dynamic process. You are the authority figure. Students who are engaged in the self-authorization process may begin to challenge authority. This is normal but uncomfortable for the target. Generally speaking, this is not personal, however personal it may feel. It is very important to respond impersonally. For example: "There seems to be some agitation [distress, upset, anger, and so on] in the conversation. Anybody want to talk about what's going on?" Your role is to encourage reasonable expression of feelings and minimize student attacks or disrespect. You can refer to the class rules. You need to think of yourself as an observer and a person who helps students talk to each other. Remember to summarize what you have heard before adding your observations or additional information.

- Do not join the conflict. Remember, your job in this situation is to observe the dynamics and label them, not to join the conflict. Take the lid off the pot before it boils over. What people really want is to be heard. Summarize what you're hearing. That typically calms things down considerably.

- If you know you will be teaching a class where conflict is inevitable and you want to use conflict as an educational tool, invite a person with good group skills to join you for that class. Group process experts can be found in student affairs, in departments of communication, and possibly in the human resources department of your institution.

- Learning to watch and use group dynamics as an educational tool is an endless process. Start where you are. If what you see doesn't make sense to you, find somebody who is an experienced facilitator to discuss the situation with you. I recommend seeking out student affairs people, but there are also many academic departments that teach about groups. Ask your friends for suggestions. Do not talk to people who are more likely to have group counseling experience because what you are doing is not counseling and counseling issues will probably confuse the process.

Resources

- If you really want to explore this topic in greater depth, search out group decision-making styles online. Many assessment tools are available that can be used to help students develop a language for addressing and resolving differences of opinion. If you don't feel comfortable participating in the clarification process as a facilitator, ask a staff member from student activities or residence life to help. Many of these people know how to use these tools. There are also potential partners in communication and business departments.
- Consider consulting a book on group dynamics. My favorite group dynamics book is *Joining Together: Group Theory and Group Skills* (Johnson & Johnson, 2013). This book organizes group process by issues and contains many exercises to illustrate each topic.

Assessment

- Make the students assess the quality of the group work as part of their final grade. I usually ask students to write a short reflection paper after completion of a group project. This allows me to find out who really did what and how satisfied with the group the individual members were. If there are different renditions of what happened that is a good subject for a meeting with the group.
- Refer to chapter 8, on learning outcomes, for possible assessment strategies.
- Remember, the key to good assessment of group skills is to identify specific behaviors that are positive contributors. You can probably develop the list from the earlier student conversations about how good groups work.

APPENDIX B

CONTEMPLATIVE PRACTICES
FOR CLASSROOM USE

We envision an education that promotes the exploration of meaning, purpose and values and seeks to serve our common human future. An education that enables and enhances personal introspection and contemplation leads to the realization of our inextricable connection to each other, opening the heart and mind to true community, deeper insight, sustainable living, and a more just society.

(The Association for Contemplative Mind in Higher Education, 2015a)

What Are Contemplative Practices?

Contemplative practices are methods used to help students consider information from a personal perspective that involves the creation of a sense of personal meaning. They are also asked to consider the implications of what they are learning in a very broad framework that includes consideration of general human welfare.

Contemplative practices are based on the information described throughout this book that integrates learning in all areas of the brain. These practices can range from very simple to very complex, and they can be used in any discipline. Simple practices include giving students time at the beginning of a class to put down their pens or tablets, close their eyes, and take a few deep breaths so that they can clear their minds before beginning to think about the subject under discussion. In other words, breathing and sitting quietly is one way to minimize distraction before beginning to learn. On a slightly more complex level, journaling is a contemplative practice. In journaling, the students can be asked to write their reaction to a subject discussed in class and explore what this information might mean to them personally. For greater structure, the professor provides questions or prompts for students to respond to, highlighting specific aspects of the topic that the professor wants each student to consider in greater depth. This type of writing is brief, is often done in class, and can be collected or not. The purpose is for students to reflect on new information and consider consequences that might emerge from the information. The approach is both empirical and subjective, asking the students to integrate what they know and what knowing this information means to them. I have often found that a brief discussion after a writing probe is very useful because it allows students to realize the range of subjectivities present in response to apparently "objective" information.

Contemplative practices serve the purpose of anchoring learning both in a personal "meaning-making" system and in the emotional and engaged aspects of the students' lives. In other words, contemplative practices consistently raise the question of why the learning matters. The meaningfulness of learning is directly related to self-authorship. Students remember and are more likely to use information learned in any course if it directly relates to their own sense of self and purpose in life (Baxter Magolda, 1999).

All contemplative practices share three anchoring principles: communion, connection, and awareness. *Communion* suggests that students are asked to discover the relationship between themselves and the information they learn. Where does their sense of self connect with this knowledge and why should they consider holding this knowledge someplace in their minds? *Connection* has a slightly different emphasis. Connection asks us how this knowledge is connected to other knowledge, to the interpersonal and ecological worlds in which we live. Communion implies looking within. Connection implies looking beyond. *Awareness* binds the other two ideas and sets us up for noticing additional connections and a broader sense of meaning. *Mindfulness* is another term often used synonymously with awareness. The purpose of all these practices is to teach students to become more aware of whatever is in their environment, to stop and take notice and desist from *multitasking*, which, I believe, is simply another term for not paying attention. Zajonc refers to this practice of mindfulness as "looking, listening and remembering" in the education of reflective scientists (Barbezat & Bush, 2014, p. 103). Mindfulness is also considered an aspect of self-management (Barbezat & Bush, p. 102). Self-management helps students stop, become aware of their reactions, and consider the consequences before they speak or act. This process of self-management also gives students time to consider multiple perspectives on whatever subject is under discussion. It is clear that the use of mindfulness practices can be tremendously valuable in any class conversation that involves controversial topics and emotional responses to those topics. Indeed, mindfulness practices make it possible to discuss difficult issues with a sense of respect, clear thinking, and focus.

The tree that appears in Figure B.1, provided by the Association for Contemplative Mind in Higher Education (ACMHE), illustrates the range of contemplative practices that have been developed thus far in the evolution of this approach to teaching and learning. As long as a professor remembers the roots and the principles of mind-body integration in learning, there is no limit to the types of contemplative practices that can be created. The trunk and the branches of the tree specify the categories of practice and the leaves are examples.

ACMHE (2015b) offers annual conferences, a summer curriculum workshop, and brief training programs in various locations around the United States. A list of resources follows:

- Barbezat, D., & Bush, M. (2013). *Contemplative practices in higher education: Powerful methods to transform teaching and learning*. San Francisco, CA: Jossey-Bass.
- Barbezat, D., & Pingree, A. (2012). Contemplative pedagogy: The special role of teaching and learning centers. In J. E. Groccia & L. Cruz (Eds.), *To improve the academy* (Vol. 31, pp. 177–191). San Francisco, CA: Jossey-Bass.
- Burggraf, S., & Grossenbacher, P. (2007, June). Contemplative modes of inquiry in liberal arts education. *LiberalArtsOnline* Retrieved from http://www.wabash.edu/news/docs/Jun07 ContemplativeModes1.pdf

- Bush, M. (2010). *Contemplative higher education in contemporary America.* Retrieved from https://mindful campus.files.wordpress.com/2012/03/mbush-contemplative highereducation.pdf
- Bush, M. (2011). Contemplative higher education in contemporary life. In M. Bush (Ed.), *Contemplation nation: How ancient practices are changing the way we live* (pp. 221–236). CreateSpace.
- Kroll, K. (Ed.). (2010). *Contemplative teaching and learning: New directions for community colleges,* No. 151. San Francisco, CA: Jossey-Bass.
- Langer, E. J. (1998). *The power of mindful learning.* Boston, MA: Da Capo Press.
- Miller, J. P. (2014). *The contemplative practitioner: Meditation in education and the workplace* (2nd ed.). Toronto, Canada: University of Toronto Press.
- Sanders, L. A. (Ed.). (2013, Summer). *Contemplative studies in higher education: New directions for teaching and learning,* No. 134.
- Shapiro, S., Brown, K. W., & Austin, J. A. (2011). Toward the integration of meditation into higher education: A review of research evidence. *Teachers College Record, 113*(3), 493–528.
- Siegel, D. J. (2007). *The mindful brain: Reflection and attunement in the cultivation of well-being.* New York, NY: W. W. Norton & Company.

Figure B.1 Categories of contemplative practices and examples.

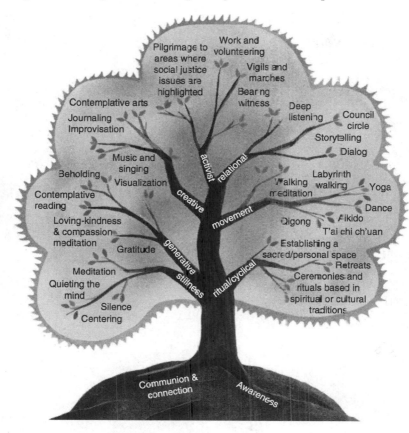

Note. Reprinted with permission from ACMHE, November 2014.

REFERENCES

Albert Einstein Quotes. (n.d.). Retrieved from http://www.brainyquote.com/quotes/authors/a/albert_einstein.html

Arum, R., & Roksa, J. (2011). *Academically adrift: Limited learning on college campuses*. Chicago, IL: University of Chicago Press.

Association for Contemplative Mind in Higher Education (ACMHE). (2015a). *Our mission*. Retrieved from http://www.contemplativemind.org/about/vision

Association for Contemplative Mind in Higher Education (ACMHE) (2015b). *Recommended reading*. Retrieved from http://www.contemplativemind.org/resources/higher-education/recommended-reading

Association of American Colleges and Universities (AAC&U). (2005). *Liberal education outcomes: A preliminary report on student achievement in college*. Washington, DC: Author.

Barbezat, D., & Bush, M. (2014). *Contemplative practices in higher education*. San Francisco, CA: Jossey-Bass.

Barker, J. (1992). *The business of discovering the future*. New York, NY: HarperCollins.

Bateson, M. (1990). *Composing a life*. New York, NY: Plume.

Baxter Magolda, M. (1999). *Creating contexts for learning and self-authorship*. Nashville, TN: Vanderbilt University Press.

Baxter Magolda, M., & King, P. (Eds.). (2004). *Learning partnerships: Theory and models of practice to educate for self-authorship*. Sterling, VA: Stylus.

Begley, S. (2007). *Train your mind to change your brain*. New York, NY: Ballantine.

Belenky, M., Clinchy, B., Goldberger, N., & Tarule, J. (1986). *Women's ways of knowing*. New York, NY: Basic Books.

Berry, T. (1999). *The great work: Our way into the future*. New York, NY: Bell Tower.

Berry, T. (2009). *The sacred universe*. New York, NY: Columbia University Press.

Bloom, A. (1987). *The closing of the American mind*. New York, NY: Touchstone.

Bohm, D. (2003). *The essential David Bohm* (L. Nichol, Ed.). New York, NY: Routledge.

Bok, D. (2006). *Our underachieving colleges*. Princeton, NJ: Princeton University Press.

Burgos, L. (2013) *Exploring students' of color leadership narratives through racial identity and pre-college experiences*. Master's Thesis. New Britain, CT: Central Connecticut State University

Caine, R., Caine, G., McClintic, C. & Klimek, K. (2005) *Brain/ mind learning principles in action*. Thousand Oaks, CA: Corwin Press.

Capra, F. (1975). *The Tao of physics*. Boston, MA: Shambhala.

Capra, F. (1982). *The turning point: Science, society and the rising of culture*. New York, NY: Scribner.

Carey, K. (2015). *The end of college: Creating the future of learning and the university of everywhere*. New York, NY: Riverhead Press.

Carroll, L. (1865/1993). *Alice's adventures in wonderland*. New York, NY: Dover.

Chávez, A., & Longerbeam, S. (2016). *Teaching across cultural strengths*. Sterling, VA: Stylus.

Chickering, A., & Reisser, L. (1993). *Education and identity* (2nd ed.). San Francisco, CA: Jossey-Bass.

Code, L. (1993). Taking subjectivity into account. In L. Alcoff & E. Potter (Eds.), *Feminist epistemologies* (pp. 15–48). New York, NY: Routledge.

Council for the Advancement of Standards in Higher Education, Strayhorn, T. L., Creamer, D. G., Miller, T. K., & Arminio, J. L. (2011). *Frameworks for assessing learning and development outcomes*. Washington, DC: Council for the Advancement of Standards in Higher Education.

Crow, M. M., & Dabars, W. B. (2015). *Designing the new American university*. Baltimore, MD: Johns Hopkins University Press.

Dr. Seuss. (1954). *Horton hears a who!* New York, NY: Random House.

Eisenstein, C. (2013). *The more beautiful world our hearts know is possible*. Berkeley, CA: North Atlantic Books.

Felten, P. (2014a). *Engaging students as partners in learning and teaching: A guide for the faculty*. San Francisco, CA: Jossey-Bass.

Felten, P. (2014b). *Transforming students: Fulfilling the promise of higher education*. Baltimore, MD: Johns Hopkins University Press.

Fogel, A., Stevenson, M., & Messenger, D. (1996). A comparison of the parent-child relationship in Japan and the United States. In

J. Roopnarine & D. Carter (Eds.), *Parent-child socialization in diverse cultures: Annual advances in applied developmental psychology* (Vol. 5, pp. 35–49). Norwood, NJ: Ablex.

Freire, P. (1990). *Pedagogy of the oppressed.* New York, NY: Continuum.

Fried, J. (1966). *De rerum naturae: On the nature of things.* Bachelor's degree thesis. Binghamton, NY: Harpur College.

Fried, J. (1995). *Shifting paradigms in student affairs.* Lanham, MD: Rowman & Littlefield.

Fried, J. (2012). *Transformative learning through engagement: Student affairs practice as experiential pedagogy.* Sterling, VA: Stylus.

Fried, J. (2013). Engaged learning: Why feelings matter. *About Campus, 18,* 2–8.

Goleman, D. (2003). *Destructive emotions: How can we overcome them?* New York, NY: Bantam.

Grande, S. (2004). *Red pedagogy.* New York, NY: Rowman & Littlefield.

Hart Research Associates. (2009, April). *Learning and assessment: Trends in undergraduate education.* Retrieved from www.aacu.org/membership/documents/2009MemberSurvey_Part1.pdf

Henderson, J. G., & Gornik, R. (2007). *Transformative curriculum leadership* (3rd ed.) Upper Saddle River, NJ: Pearson

Herman, A. (2013). *The cave and the light.* New York, NY: Random House.

Higher Education Research Brief. (2013, January). *Your first college year survey, 2012.* Los Angeles, CA: Cooperative Institutional Research Program.

Higher Education Research Brief. (2014, March). *The American freshman: National norms,* Fall 2013. Los Angeles, CA: Cooperative Institutional Research Program.

Johnson, D., & Johnson, F. (2013). *Joining together: Group theory and group skills* (11th ed.). Minneapolis, MN: Pearson.

Kabat-Zinn, J. (2012). *Mindfulness for beginners.* Boulder, CO: Sounds True.

Kant, I. (1979). *Conflict of the faculties* (Der streit der fakultaten) M. Gergor, Trans.). New York, NY: Abaris Books. (Original work published 1798)

Keeling, R. P. (2008). Educators, service providers, or both? *CACUSS Communiqué, 8*(2), 4–8.

Kegan, R. (1994). *In over our heads: The mental demands of modern life.* Cambridge, MA: Harvard University Press.

Kegan, R. (2000). What "form" transforms? A constructive-developmental approach to transformative learning. In J. Mezirow (Ed.), *Learning as transformation* (pp. 35–70). San Francisco, CA: Jossey-Bass.

Keller, E. (1983). *A feeling for the organism: The life of Barbara McClintock.* New York, NY: Henry Holt.

References

King, P., & Kitchener, K. (1994). *Developing reflective judgment*. San Francisco, CA: Jossey-Bass.

Komives, S., & Smedick, W. (2012). Using standards to develop student learning outcomes. *New Directions for Student Services, 140*, 77–88.

Kuh, G. (2011). *Promising practices in student engagement and retention*. Bloomington, IN: Center for Postsecondary Research, Indiana University.

Kuhn, T. (1996). *The structure of scientific revolutions* (3rd ed.). Chicago, IL: University of Chicago Press.

Laszlo, E. (2006). *The chaos point: The world at the crossroads*. Charlottesville, VA: Hampton Roads.

Love, P., & Estanek, S. (2004). *Rethinking student affairs practice*. San Francisco, CA: Jossey-Bass.

Lovelock, J. (2009). *The vanishing face of Gaia*. New York, NY: Basic Books.

Maki, P. (2004). *Assessing for learning*. Sterling, VA: Stylus.

Mezirow, J., & Associates. (2000). *Learning as transformation*. San Francisco, CA: Jossey-Bass.

Milne, A. (1926/1954). *The complete Winnie the Pooh*. New York, NY: E.P. Dutton.

National Association of Student Personnel Administrators (NASPA) & American College Personnel Association (ACPA). (2004). Learning reconsidered: A campus-wide focus on the student experience. Retrieved from https://www.naspa.org/images/uploads/main/Learning_Reconsidered_Report.pdf

Ogbu, J. (1990). Cultural models, identity and literacy. In R. Stigler, R. Schweder, & G. Herdt (Eds.), *Cultural psychology* (pp. 520–541). New York, NY: Columbia University Press.

Palmer, P., & Zajonc, A. (2010). *The heart of higher education: A call to renewal*. San Francisco, CA: Jossey-Bass.

Parks, S. (2000). *Big questions, worthy dreams*. San Francisco, CA: Jossey-Bass.

Peddiwell, J. (1939). *The saber-tooth curriculum*. New York, NY: McGraw-Hill.

Perry, W. (1968). *Forms of intellectual and ethical development in the college years*. New York, NY: Rinehart and Winston.

Polanyi, M. (1966). *The tacit dimension*. New York, NY: Doubleday.

Readings, B. (1996). *The university in ruins*. Cambridge, MA: Harvard University Press.

Sarton, M. (1973). *Journal of a solitude*. New York, NY: W.W. Norton.

Shaull, R. (1990). Forward. In P. Freire, *Pedagogy of the oppressed* (pp. 9–15). New York, NY: Continuum.

Sibley, B. (Ed.). (1986). *The Pooh book of quotations*. New York, NY: Dutton Children's Books.

Siegel, D. (2007). *The mindful brain.* New York, NY: W.W. Norton.

Stevens, W. (1964). *The collected poems of Wallace Stevens.* New York, NY: Knopf.

Stookey, S. (2012). Teaching for transformation in business education: Student affairs practice as experiential pedagogy. In J. Fried (Ed.), *Transformative learning through engagement* (pp. 153–160). Sterling, VA: Stylus.

The Editors of the Encyclopaedia Britannica (2015). *Charles William Elliot: American educator.* Retrieved from http://www.britann.ca.com/biography/Charles-William-Eliot

Vygotsky, L. S. (1991). *The Vygotsky reader* (R. van der Veer & J. Valsiner, Eds.). Cambridge, MA: Blackwell.

Watts, A. (1969). *The book: On the taboo against knowing who you are.* New York, NY: Random House.

Wheatley, M. (1999). *Leadership and the new science.* San Francisco, CA: Berrett-Koehler.

Wood, G. (2014, September). The future of college? *Atlantic.* Retrieved from http://www.theatlantic.com/magazine/archive/2014/09/the-future-of-college/375071/

Wordsworth, W. (1798). The tables turned: An evening scene on the same subject. In M. H. Abrams (Ed.), *The Norton anthology of English literature, Volume 2: The romantic period through the twelfth century* (Norton Anthology of English Literature) (8th ed., pp. 67–125). New York, NY: W.W. Norton & Co.

Yoakum, C. (1994). Plan for a personnel bureau in educational institutions. In A. L. Rentz (Ed.), *Student affairs: A profession's heritage* (2nd ed., pp. 4–8). Lanham, MD: University Press of America/American College Personnel Association.

Zull, J. (2002). *The art of changing the brain.* Sterling, VA: Stylus.

ABOUT THE AUTHORS

Jane Fried, PhD, is a professor in the Department of Counselor Education and Family Therapy at Central Connecticut State University. She is the former coordinator of the student development in higher education master's degree program. Dr. Fried is the author of *Transformative Learning Through Engagement: Student Affairs Practice as Experiential Pedagogy* and *Shifting Paradigms in Student Affairs* (Stylus, 2012), as well as coauthor of *Understanding Diversity: A Learning-as-Practice Primer* (Wadsworth, 1998). She was also one of the primary authors in *Learning Reconsidered 1* and *2* (ACPA, ACUHO-I, NACADA, NACA, NASPA, & NIRSA, 2004; 2006) and has written several monographs on ethics in student affairs and student development education. She currently writes a blog (https://hjf205 wordpress.com/author/hjf205jane/), where her primary topics of concern are racism and transformative learning, and hosts diversity dialogues to support leaders in higher education who want to develop a deeper understanding of the ways that racism affects our society.

Peter F. Troiano, PhD, is an assistant professor in the Department of Counselor Education and Family Therapy at Central Connecticut State University. Dr. Troiano has served as vice president for student and university affairs and dean of students at Southern Connecticut State University and as vice president for student affairs and dean of students at Mitchell College. His primary area of research interest is college students with learning disabilities. He has published articles in both the *Journal of College Student Development* and the *Journal of Reading and Learning*. Dr. Troiano currently serves as chair of the Professional Standards Division for Region I NASPA (National Association for Student Personnel Administrators) and representative to the national Professional Standards Division of NASPA.

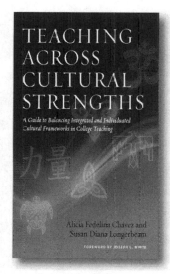

Teaching Across Cultural Strengths

A Guide to Balancing Integrated and Individuated Cultural Frameworks in College Teaching

Alicia Fedelina Chávez and Susan Diana Longerbeam

Foreword by Joseph L. White

"*Teaching Across Cultural Strengths* is an important book that can transform college teaching. It provides a breakthrough approach to addressing the urgent problem of how to teach effectively to an increasingly multicultural and international student body now enrolling in our colleges and universities. Beginning with an important question, 'How does my culture manifest itself in my teaching?,' the authors take us on a journey of self-discovery. Their objective is to explain why and how to 'balance the application of diverse cultural strengths to deepen student learning through enhancement of teaching and introspection.' The results are a book filled with rich insights, techniques, best practices, and personal stories of success about what works to engage both students and faculty in college classrooms today."—**Roberto Ibarra**, *Associate Professor, Department of Sociology and Criminology, University of New Mexico*

"This . . . brilliant and engaging . . . book has the potential to literally change the face of college teaching and learning from a multicultural perspective. No one who reads this text and reflects on its message can continue to teach in the old monocultural ways of teaching and learning."—**Joseph L. White**, *Professor Emeritus of Psychology and Psychiatry, University of California, Irvine*

22883 Quicksilver Drive
Sterling, VA 20166-2102

Subscribe to our e-mail alerts: www.Styluspub.com

Also available from Stylus

Transformative Learning Through Engagement
Student Affairs Practice as Experiential Pedagogy
Jane Fried
Foreword by James E. Zull

"This book examines the important role student affairs professionals can and should play in teaching and learning. As colleges and universities adapt to the new realities of higher education (including new understandings about how people learn), student affairs professionals can provide experiential learning opportunities that help students cross inter- and intrapersonal borders. With discussions of dominant paradigms and cultures within U.S. contexts and examples of a range of campus applications, this book provides a framework for thinking about student affairs as key to college learning, particularly in areas related to diversity. It is a useful tool for student affairs professionals working to contribute to the educational missions of the twenty-first century."—*Diversity & Democracy*

"Anyone who selects education as a career will find this book both illuminating and affirming. Examples of the roles student affairs can play in helping to structure integrated learning and Jane Fried's practical and in-depth explanation of how learning occurs make this book an excellent primer for new professionals and an essential reference book for all others. It confirms the assertion upon which the popular *Learning Reconsidered* is based: 'The most important factor is that transformative learning always occurs in the active context of students' lives.' Teaching from the perspective of what one learns from this book, especially about diversity and citizenship, will help educators eliminate the one question that every student has asked at some time: 'Why do I have to take this course?' This book is a winner!"—*Gwen Dungy, Executive Director, NASPA*

(Continues on previous page)